SMASH IT

Raise your performance with the techniques used
by top entrepreneurs and athletes

DAVID HAIMES

Powerhouse Publications
Suite 124. 94 London Road
Headington, Oxford
OX3 9FN

www.powerhousepublishing.com

TESTIMONIALS

"This is a great read if you really want fulfil your full potential, either in sport, in work or in your personal life. I highly recommend that you not only read it but implement all the techniques it teaches you."

– Chris Robshaw.
Rugby Player. Former Captain of England.

"I love to the help people I meet in life. Now my task is much easier by just recommending this book. Everyone can get something valuable from David's clear and compelling advice."

– Baroness Sheehan,
British politician and life peer.

ACKNOWLEDGEMENTS

I would like to thank my wonderful wife Annie. Without her amazing support and encouragement I would never have achieved the life we have today.

I would also like to thank my amazing colleagues and clients that inspire me every day with their passion, endeavour and endless energy. I am sure I learn as much from you, as you do from me!

CONTENTS

INTRODUCTION

If Only I Could?

Take a moment to reflect on the proudest achievements in your life so far.

Winning that race, passing that exam, marrying that wonderful man or woman, having your first beautiful child, getting that exciting promotion, starting that amazing company.

Those times that you were in perfect flow, you were invincible and life felt joyful and effortless.

Now ask yourself, how many times are you hitting those peaks now? How much of the rest of your time is spent being distinctly average?

Then ask yourself, 'What if I could perform at that level all of the time, or at least most of the time?' Your performance would be absolutely awesome.

If only I could…?

Do you ever look at other people around you: people who are performing amazing things?
Do you look at them in envy and think, 'Wow, how do they perform at that level consistently?'
What does that level of performance bring to their lives?
They must be leading a richer life than me.
How could I learn how to achieve at that level?

If only I could…?

Then you look at some of the areas of your life that you are not so happy with.
Maybe the times when you are telling yourself that you want to exercise more.

I want to feel better.

I want to eat better.

I want to look better.

Even though I try in these areas, often with great bursts of enthusiasm, I never seem able to keep it up to a level that helps me be that person.

If only I could…?

When you are playing some of your most important roles in life; being a parent or being a wife or a husband or a boss. You know that sometimes you do perform really well in these roles. However, for large amounts of time you are distracted by other things.

Are there times when you look at yourself and say, 'I could do better than that'?

Do you think to yourself that if I were consistent and performed at my best in those really important roles, my life would be better?

If only I could…?

The good news is that you can.

Because those other people that you look at in envy are ordinary people just like you. They are absolutely no different. No more clever. No more talented. No more lucky.

The only difference between them and you is that they have learned a set of skills and habits that allow them to perform at their best over long periods of time in multiple roles.

Hence, their level of achievement is much higher over the course of their lives, than yours is.

The second piece of good news is that you can learn these things too. They are really not difficult.

This book is dedicated to learning just those things.

If you like what's in this book, and you apply what's in this book, the level of your achievement will rise dramatically.

The answer to:

If only I could... is: YOU CAN.

Do it now.

BEFORE WE START

Asking the right question?

Having been a professional business coach for some time now, it is clear to me that most people at some point in their lives stop learning how to improve their performance at work, at home or both.

We plateau. We stall. Our progress towards reaching our full potential slows down or grinds to a halt.

Sometimes we just never get personal growth momentum in the first place.

Our personal potential lies dormant waiting for someone or something to wake it up again.

There are lots of reasons why this occurs. We will not explore those reasons in this book as that would involve us dwelling in the past.

This is a forward-looking book. Its focus is 100% on your exciting future, not your past.

Whatever the reason is that you are not on track to reach your full potential, the remedy is exactly the same – hence your own personal reasons are totally irrelevant and we will choose to leave them behind.

When this happens, we ask ourselves lots of questions. Most of them are around: *what do I need to do next to get what I want?*

- Should I work harder?
- Should I change jobs?
- Should I change profession?
- Should I change my relationships?
- Should I train harder?
- Should I take up Yoga?

- Should I change my image?
- Should I buy a different car?
- Should I tell my horrible boss where to go, and start my own business?
- Should I move to a different country where the weather is better and life will be easier?
- Should I read more books on success?

The answers to these questions are so often not clear in our heads. In fact, we are not even sure if these are the right questions. We spend lots of time and energy experimenting with these thoughts. We test some or all of them to see what happens. There are lots of false starts. We procrastinate and struggle to make decisions. It feels like every time we take one step forward it's followed by taking two steps backwards.

Does any of this sound familiar to you?

The underlying reason for the struggle is that there is no real context around these thoughts because we are asking ourselves the wrong questions.

A much better question is:

Who am I capable of being?

You have achieved lots of great things in life so far when it's been clear to you what you needed to achieve and the outcome is desirable to you.

You have also demonstrated your ability to master a load of new skills in order to achieve those goals.

So, what if you applied this energy and capacity to learn to becoming *the person* you could be?

You could probably become anyone you wanted to be. How exciting is that?

So, life becomes clearer as soon as you decide who you want to BE.

Decisions and actions become much easier within this context.

I will share with you a few of the things I want to **BE** as an example.

I want to BE:

- A great father to my four kids.
- A great husband for my wonderful wife.
- A great coach and mentor for talented business owners.
- A recognised leader in the field of performance coaching.
- A great speaker on stage.
- An accomplished author.
- An energetic and healthy person who loves life every single day.

Asking yourself WHO you need to be and learning how to be that person is much more fun and fulfilling than chasing things that you think you should do to get what you think you want.

Once you are crystal clear on *who* you want to BE, what you need to do just falls into place naturally.
The fog clears and decisions become easy again.
Decisions lead to actions.
Actions lead to performance.
Performance leads to progress and personal growth.

There is a calmness of mind knowing that whilst there will be many milestones along the way, the fun is in the journey NOT in achieving any end point. So, it does not feel like a race to gain anything in the material sense, but more like an amazing journey with loads of interesting twists and turns along the way.

In common with any journey, there are still plenty of low moments where you don't live up to your desired version of yourself – but knowing the context within which you are travelling gets you back on track pretty quickly.

So, what I am proposing is to redefine your definition of personal 'success' into becoming the person you want to be.

The consequences of this are immense:

- Success for you can only be framed by **you**…no-one else.
- It's very personal. Only you know if you achieve it or are on the right journey towards it.
- If you have the personal conviction to follow this path then you can design your own future and be in control of your own destiny.
- What other people judge you on is now totally **irrelevant**. You are writing your own story… and they don't know the script.

Your journey starts from here, should you choose to entertain this thinking.
Start asking yourself who you want to be.
Start making some notes.

HOW to become that person?

It is not just the discovery of asking yourself the right question that I wanted to share with you, although this idea in itself is momentous enough to change your life; It is what I have observed and learned about the process of HOW to become the person you want to be.

The first thing I am asking you to accept now is that everyone can be who they want to be. Without this mindset, then you simply can't get there. You just allow yourself to accept too many excuses and create a set of self-limiting beliefs.

All the evidence backs up this thinking. Most extraordinary people are simply not born, they are made from ordinary people who decide to become extraordinary and learn how to do it.

You have the same opportunity as everyone else.

Superheroes are made not born

In my profession, I am lucky enough to work with some amazing people who are performing at the top of their game, really being the person who they have chosen to be.

As an avid student of the art and science of performance-coaching I love to hear their stories.

They all have a few things in common.

Whilst they all undoubtedly have characteristics that stem from their genetic make-up and their early upbringing, it was not these factors that enabled them to achieve what they have achieved. It is a set of learned skills and habits that they have decided to learn and put in the hard yards to perfect. They all worked very hard to attain a high degree of competency in areas that they selected as being key to achieving their goals.

I am lucky enough to work with some of the coaches and athletes from GB Rowing. These guys are at the top of their sport and they know a thing or two about building high performance individuals and teams. GB Rowing is one of the most successful of our Olympic teams and consistently performs on the world's biggest sporting stage. I have learnt a lot from them. One of their key beliefs is that mind-set and hard work builds high performance, not the degree of natural talent you are born with.

Now, don't get me wrong. There are some clear limitations in this thinking. If, genetically, it is deemed you are going to be five feet in height then it's unlikely you will become a world-class basketball player, no matter how dedicated you are to learning these skills.

However, outside of a relatively small list of genetic limitations there is still a massive amount of scope remaining for all the things you could become.

So, genetics are just not a limiting factor to becoming the best version of yourself that you can imagine.

In fact, there is strong evidence to suggest the most gifted people from a genetic sense have a distinct disadvantage. The mere fact that they are able to perform effortlessly better than their peers at a relatively early age prevents them developing the learning habits and work ethic required to constantly improve. Then gradually they get left behind, left ill-equipped to compete.

I was lucky enough to attend a coaching seminar given by the great athletics coach Frank Dick OBE. Frank has coached some amazing sport stars such as Daley Thompson and is currently working with Eddie Jones and England Rugby.

He was telling us that in sport it's often the kids who come second or third in early trials who are chosen for the high-performance academies and go on to lead their sports.

Also, he explained that it is no accident that a disproportionate number of highly-successful people are dyslexic as they had to work really hard to keep up at school.

This is because the drive and determination required to learn new skills and develop performance habits always trumps 'natural talent'.

Then there is the issue of background. If you are born into extreme poverty or into a war-zone then the mere act of survival is a victory. Conversely, if you are born into a ruling dynasty then choosing not to play your destined role can be a severe limitation. However, outside some of these extremes, your background does not preclude you from becoming who you choose to be.

Even if you are struggling to accept that you can be ANYTHING you want to be, you must at least accept that you can certainly be the BEST possible version of yourself.

So, if you can imagine a better version of yourself, then read on.

Thousands of people every day, in every part of the globe, thrive on travelling this well-trodden path. My coaching colleagues and I have guided many people over the years. Throughout this book I hope to be your guide to enable you to follow in their footsteps and help you build your path to some incredible personal achievements that you perhaps have not even dreamed of yet.

Understanding the process of change

Before you embark on this journey there are a couple of things you need to think about in advance to orientate yourself.

As you are reading this book, I am assuming that, you don't want to stand still. You have decided that you want to make some changes in your life.

Change does not come easy to most. We all have an inbuilt resistance to change that needs to be overcome to make progress and build momentum.

You will need three things to overcome your own natural resistance:

1. Firstly, you need a **degree of dissatisfaction** with where you are right now. I am guessing you have a least some of this if you have purchased this book? The point being that if you are satisfied with where you are, then you are unlikely to have the energy and determination to make the changes needed to create a better you.

   If you are happy with where you are, but still want to explore all the possibilities available to you then this is still a good mindset. By envisioning new possibilities that excite you, then dissatisfaction will grow naturally anyway.

   It's like when I bought my first mountain bike: I loved it with a passion until my ability grew and I started to ride with better riders with better bikes. Then I became dissatisfied with my once-loved machine. This new feeling of dissatisfaction gave me the determination and desire to earn a bit more money to buy a better machine and become a better rider. To scratch the dissatisfaction itch.

2. Secondly, you will need to develop a **vision of your future self**; a vision that really excites you. If you are not satisfied with where you are and have a clear and compelling vision of where you want to go, then you have the ingredients required to start the change process.

   Going back to the big question, can you vividly imagine your future self and are you really excited by getting there?

   For me personally, I have the images in my mind of the experiences I want with my children and my wife; I can see myself celebrating breakthroughs with my coaching clients; I can see and feel the applause as I come off stage after a speaking event; and I can picture signing copies of my new best-selling book.

   It's a clear and attainable enough set of images that help me do what I need to do every day to take another step along my journey.

3. Lastly, you will need to **know how to take the next step** to make change actually happen. Dissatisfaction and vision give you the desire to change, but that's no good if you don't know **how** to do it.

   However, you don't need to know everything required to take you all the way to your destination. Knowing the first steps for each area of your life that you want to change is enough to get started and build momentum.

   For some of us, this is a difficult idea (particularly for the planners and control freaks). The thought of starting on a journey without a fully planned route map, with every step worked out, can be a really scary. However, this need to know everything often creates such a complex picture that the whole idea becomes so daunting that you **never start in the first place**. So, what is better: starting the journey and trusting that your guide will help you with every step, or not starting at all?

Most successful people have mentors/coaches around them who they trust to guide them and hold them accountable for the goals they set themselves. The mere fact that they have this support allows them to focus on the next step, confident in the knowledge that their mentor/coach has the path mapped out.

Remember that momentum is everything, once you get positive momentum fueled by a number of wins and celebrations then your journey has truly started. It's like the flywheel that starts to spin... Once it's in motion it takes a lot to stop it.

So, the first steps might be things as simple as:

Re-organizing your week to place the really high-value activities in pole position.
or
Spending some quality time on a goal-setting exercise to set new and exciting goals for yourself.
or
Booking your next three holidays.
or
Hiring a Personal Trainer

Simple stuff that sets you on your way.

This approach to making change happen is often summarized in what's been termed 'the formula for change':

$$(D \times V) + F > R$$

Where D is Dissatisfaction
V is Vision
F is First Steps
And R is Resistance to change.

The biggest factors causing resistance to change are:
Comfort - You are too comfortable to find the energy to roll the dice.
Fear - You are scared of the implications of change.
Uncertainty - You struggle to make decisions on things that are not certain.
Doubt - You doubt your own ability to achieve more.

If you suffer for any of these, then I would ask you to write down two lists:

1. list the worst things that could happen if you attempt to raise your game and stride forward in pursuit of finding your full potential.
2. list the best things that could happen to you if you took this path.

If the second list does not excite you more than the anxiety of the first list, then go no further. You are not cut out for the journey.
For most of you the second list will be much stronger and the risk-reward equation will be heavily weighted to moving forward with confidence and conviction.

However, before you start, ask yourself where you sit with regard to this formula. You probably have some degree of all three of the factors that will give you the forward momentum to overcome your resistance to change. If you are unsure if your personal factors are strong enough, don't worry. By the end of the book these factors will all be significantly higher.

The bad news

Up to now you might be thinking this all sounds easy and you can't wait to get going. However, I would be leading you up the garden path if I did not tell you about the tough bits: the self-discipline, hard work and persistence required to make change stick.

What we are talking about is improving our personal performance in the areas of our lives that are important to us. This involves learning new skills, behaviours and habits. Developing new ways of thinking.

Now, we can all adapt our thinking and behaviour for a short period of time. Stop drinking for a few days, going to the gym for a couple of weeks, organizing our key meetings for a month. However, this does nothing to bring about the long lasting and truly positive change we want.

For the new skills and behaviours to stick, they need to become habits.

New habits require the repetition of tasks over and over until the new behaviour is not only learned, but you become 'unconsciously competent' at the new skill. You can perform it seemingly automatically without consciously thinking about it.

When you watch Roger Federer serve in a seemingly effortless manner you never see the thousands of times he has practised this exact action to the point that his body can repeat it perfectly in a competitive environment without thinking. This allows him to be thinking about how to handle the return of service at that moment in time, not the serve.

However, so often when we attempt to acquire new skills our initial enthusiasm is short-lived, our good intentions get chipped away by those inevitable thoughts and emotions that creep in, such as:

- 'It's just one day, one drink, one exception. I will get back with it tomorrow.'
- 'I am too tired to pull my trainers on and go for a run this morning...besides it looks like it could rain.'
- 'I know what I need to do this week, no need to plan my schedule in advance.'

This creep turns into apathy until the enthusiasm drops away and the new habit is abandoned way before it has had the chance to get established.

To master the new habits, we have to learn the art of controlling our thoughts.

In other words, we have to find a high degree of self-discipline whilst we are practising our new skills. This self-discipline needs to be applied for a long enough period for the new activity to become a habit. Once it becomes a habit the level of mental effort to perform the task is minimal. It becomes a learned skill that can be performed automatically.

We must learn how to train our brain to control the natural emotions that will sabotage the new habits we want to master.

Now this is far from easy, but with practice we can all learn how to do this.

To be 100% crystal clear up front:

Yes, it requires a lot of self-discipline (controlling our thoughts) to stick with the activity until it becomes a habit.
Yes, it requires hard work to repeat the activity sometimes thousands of times until the new skill/behaviour can be repeated perfectly without having to think about how to do it.
Yes is requires persistence to battle through the days when either your mind or body is telling you it really is not up for it.

But all the effort makes the results taste so sweet.

The focus and effort transforms ordinary people into extraordinary people, into superheroes.

Keeping simple things simple

The good news is that learning habits to improve your personal performance is not complicated. It's not easy but it's not complicated.

Through carefully observing the high-performance individuals from the worlds of business and sport that I have had the privilege to work with and been lucky enough to coach, I have found that they all, without exception, excel in three core areas. By learning the skills and habits in these three areas, I am 100% confident anyone can raise their performance to the level they need to hit the goals they set for themselves.

The first area is *self-mastery*. This is about training your mind and body to be capable to perform at a higher level.

The second I call *connectivity*. These are the skills and habits that allow you to attract and surround yourself with like-minded, talented people who will help you reach your goals.

The third is *personal productivity*. This is where you learn how to get the very best out of every day, allowing you to achieve much more with less time.

The rest of this book is dedicated to exploring why these areas drive performance, what these specific skills and habits are that can be learnt, and how you can learn them.

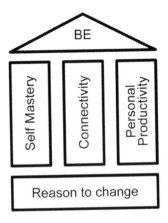

How to get the best from this book

Learning to raise your personal performance is an active, not passive, activity.

To get the best from the book, you will need to turn new thoughts into new actions. Otherwise, your investment in time and money will just be rewarded by a dose of education and entertainment rather than any real performance increases.

So, every section asks you reflective questions and will invite you to set yourself goals backed by concrete activities that will help you develop the skills and habits that will lead you along your chosen journey.

The more you participate, the more you will make progress.

It does not matter which section of the content you are working on at any one time… every section adds value in isolation. When you can master all sections in harmony, then you will have moved to a new level of performance.

So, before we get started let's reflect a little by completing the **BE baseline assessment.**

Please be 100% honest with yourself… delusion and denial helps nobody.

What areas of your life are working really well and you don't want to change?

```



```

What areas of your life are you dissatisfied with?

```
┌─────────────────────────────────────────────────────────┐
│                                                           │
│                                                           │
│                                                           │
│                                                           │
│                                                           │
└─────────────────────────────────────────────────────────┘
```

What are the dreams you have for yourself? Who could you be?

```
┌─────────────────────────────────────────────────────────┐
│                                                           │
│                                                           │
│                                                           │
│                                                           │
│                                                           │
└─────────────────────────────────────────────────────────┘
```

What would be the impact on your life, and those close to you if you became this person?

```
┌─────────────────────────────────────────────────────────┐
│                                                           │
│                                                           │
│                                                           │
│                                                           │
│                                                           │
└─────────────────────────────────────────────────────────┘
```

Thanks for your participation so far. Now let's get to work.

PART ONE

SELF-MASTERY

Self-Mastery

Many of us become very focused of working on our businesses, our jobs, our homes etc., but for some strange reason forget to work on ourselves.

Our minds and bodies are the tools we use for everything we do in life. The better condition we keep them in, the better we are able to perform at our best.

First work on yourself – then work on your job.

I often hear people saying that they don't have time to read, or to eat well, reflect or exercise properly. They are just too busy!

To raise our own performance, this is the first paradigm that has to be reversed.

High performers know it requires a fit mind and fit body to perform at their best and they work harder on this than any other aspects of their lives. We all know this deep down, but just get too distracted on other aspects of our lives to act on this belief.

Your mind and body work in a totally interdependent manner. Your body will not perform unless your mind is strong and agile, your mind will not perform unless your body is strong and agile. Both have to be in great working order, and in balance, to attain and sustain performance at a high level.

We all know when we are in good shape; we have energy, we are thinking clearly, we look good and we feel good.
The opposite is true when we don't work hard enough on ourselves.

So where do you begin to train your mind and body to get in shape, and stay in shape, to perform at your best?

In working with the amazing people I am lucky enough to be coaching, or have coached, I have observed four areas which, when strong and well-maintained keep them in great shape.

Through working on these areas, you can learn how to systematically stay in top form.

These are:

$$Purpose + Identity + Progressive\ Mindset + Energy = Fitness$$
to perform at your best.

Purpose is the force that drives you to strive to achieve something.
Identity is the future self you have designed for yourself.
Progressive Mindset is a way of thinking that consistently creates successful progress towards achieving a purpose.
Energy is creating a balance between the activities you do that maintain the mind and body in a fresh and energetic state which allows you to perform consistently at high levels over long periods of time.

In this section I hope to give you an easy-to-follow framework to develop good habits in each of these areas. This is the starting point for raising your game and I am confident you will see immediate benefits from working on yourself in this way.

Finding your purpose

Most of us normal humans require a reason to do the hard yards it takes to reach our full potential.

The reality is that 99.9 % of us settle for doing enough to survive or live a comfortable life. It's only a few that ask the question of what they are fully capable of AND then actively pursue the answer.

You are one of the few, otherwise you would not be reading this book.

We have all heard stories of extraordinary people who achieved extraordinary things. These people achieved not because they could, but because they had a compelling reason to do so. Without this compelling reason, you don't have the drive and determination to overcome the inevitable obstacles that lie between you today and your better future self.

For some, this purpose is dealt to them in life through circumstance. They are born as the head of a family, or a nation, etc.

For most, it requires a mental quest to find a purpose for our lives that sits well above the defaults for living in the society in which we are born and bought up in.

To become the person you want to be you have to go on this journey and find an answer that will sustain you on the hard and treacherous path to its realisation.

I say an answer because for many this purpose evolves and sometimes transforms. But without a compelling purpose that serves you for the foreseeable future you will just not have the focus, tenacity and resilience to achieve anything exceptional.

Purpose has a number of levels.
Firstly, what achievement gives to **you.**
Secondly, what achievement gives to your **family and friends.**
Thirdly, how achievement benefits **people outside your circle,** both now and in the immediate future.
Lastly, how achievement can leave a **legacy** that benefits people for long after you have passed away.

The higher the level of purpose you have, the stronger your driving force is.

As purpose will drive performance, then it makes sense to look deep into our own hearts and minds to seek a meaningful purpose. The better the purpose we find, the stronger the force and the higher the level of performance we can reach.

At the highest level, there are many great examples of people with a clear and powerful purpose that have changed the lives of millions forever.

One of my heroes is Nelson Mandela. He had a powerful, unfaltering purpose to create a free society in South Africa. Such was his passion for this purpose, he was able to endure the most extreme mental and physical hardships to achieve it.

> *'Do not judge me by my successes, judge me by*
> *how many times I fell down and got back up*
> *again.'* – Nelson Mandela

In every word and deed, he promoted his purpose – which eventually led to the seismic changes in South African society.

Abraham Lincoln is another leader whose achievements were led by a profound sense of purpose.

His purpose was to preserve the greatest democracy the world had ever known. This was summed up in this quote from the Gettysburg Address on November 19, 1863, on the battlefield near Gettysburg, Pennsylvania:

> *"Government of the people, by the people, for*
> *the people, shall not perish from the earth."*
> – Abraham Lincoln.

Tied to the conviction that his work was intrinsically important, it was Lincoln who consistently found the courage to invigorate the spirits of his cabinet and troops during the country's most dire and desperate hours.

Whilst these are somewhat historical examples, the implications of them still live with us today.

For us mere mortals, however, it's difficult to relate such lofty examples to our lives.

So, let's start by rekindling all those dreams we have had in the past.

Let's brush them off and put them back on the table with a renewed sense of hope and enthusiasm. Then for each dream, let's ask ourselves the question. Why do we want that?

Sub-consciously there is a "Why?" behind most dreams.

Let me give you some examples from my own experiences when asking clients the simple question: **What do you really want in life?**

Dream One

Julie's dream.

"I want all of my children to go to great schools and universities. I can see them all in caps and gowns graduating. I will be so proud of them."

When asked, "Why do you want this?" and after a lot of digging deep, the true reason was revealed. It was grounded in her belief that as a child she was not given access to good education. Her parents did not have either the financial resources or see the importance in good education. Sub-consciously this created an underlying feeling of being 'let down' by her parents. This feeling of resentment was amplified by the fact that her brother was supported through education for reasons that she never really understood. So, in reality, her "Why?" was being driven substantially by the fear that her children would look back at her with the same feeling of being let down. She wanted her children to have what she was never able to have.

Interestingly, after this discussion Julie told me that she had never spoken about this to anyone because no one had ever asked. People just assumed that she believed in the value of education as a principle. But underneath, her "Why?" was much stronger than that. So strong, in fact, that she found the determination to build her own business and finance all her children through private education and university.

The other interesting fact was that until our discussion, she herself had never brought this purpose to the surface. Now that she consciously understood and could openly talk about her "Why?", the driving force became much stronger. She was able to share it with others, which in turn had two consequences. Firstly, the fact she had publicly stated to friends and family what she was going to do transformed the desire into an implied commitment, one that she could now not fall short of. Secondly, people around her related to her "Why?" and were more prepared to support her on her quest.

This example arguably plays in the first two boxes of strength. Her purpose was about self. She did not want her children to feel the resentment that she felt towards her parents. However, she also wanted her children to have the best chance in life and was prepared to sacrifice a great deal for them.

Dream Two

Joshua's dream.

"I want to build the biggest equipment hire company in our area to become a millionaire by the time I am 35."

When I asked him why he wanted this, he was not very forthcoming at first.

So, we started exploring some of the possible reasons. However, the obvious reasons that others would naturally assume quickly fell away. When asked about the lifestyle that that achievement would buy, he seemed disinterested. Then when asked about houses, cars, holidays, he seemed disinterested. When I asked about the recognition he would get from his peer group, he was somewhat oblivious of the concept of either status or ego.

It was only when we started talking about his background and his family that I saw a spark in his eyes. It turned out that he had arrived in England with his parents from the Philippines when he was four years old. His parents worked tirelessly in low-skilled jobs for many years to pay for his education. He now wanted, more than anything else, to pay them back and to give them the quality of life he felt they deserved in recognition of their sacrifices. In addition to this, he was the oldest son and therefore the de facto head of the family now. This was a role he took very seriously. In his own mind it was his responsibility to look after his extended family both here and in his hometown of Manila. It became crystal clear that the objective of growing his business and becoming a millionaire by the time he was 35 was not for himself at all, it was so that he could fulfill his role within the family.

His real purpose was to provide for the extended family and to act as a role model for his siblings and cousins to aspire to, so future generations of his family would also thrive.

The person he wanted to be was very clear in his mind and he worked hard every day to ensure he became that person. In fact, the skills and habits that he learned in striving to become this person took him well beyond his original aspirations. He is now a very successful person in so many dimensions and I am sure he will leave a strong legacy for his family and many others who are lucky enough to become his friend.

So, this level of purpose certainly ticks all four boxes in some way, although the source of his purpose originated in what he could give to his family and friends. The fact is that striving for this actually helped him become a 'superhero' and in doing so it sent ripples across all four levels of purpose. So, in many ways, it does not matter what the source of your purpose is. It matters only that the purpose is strong enough to pull you through the process of learning the skills and habits that enable you to become a high performer who is then able to have a positive impact on the lives of many other people around you.

Dream Three

Sofia's dream.

"I want to become a doctor in our local community."

When I asked this young lady why, her answer was clear and concise.

"Because my grandfather was a doctor and he has been the biggest influence in my life. He inspired me to follow in his footsteps. I want to make him and my parents very proud of what I can become."

She beamed at me with a magical smile as she said these words. It was clear that as she spoke, she was conjuring up the image of her future self on the wards of Guy's Hospital in her mind. Also, the portrait of the wrinkled face of her grandfather with a wry smile of approval and pride across his cheeks.

I knew instantly from the intensity of the look on her face that her purpose was very strong. It would be the driving force that would help her safely through her endless studies and long, grueling days as a junior doctor. It was not a complex or superhuman purpose. It was simple and beautiful.

I wanted to include this example as I have learned that often, the underlying purpose a person needs to drive them towards a goal and sustain them along the journey does not have to be anything that others may consider exceptional or inspirational. Your purpose only has to be meaningful to you and the reasons that it's powerful only have to make sense to you.

Do not feel that you have to go away on a month-long retreat in a far-away ancient monastery to find your true inner meaning! Most of the time you can dust off your dreams and say to yourself: "Why not? What's stopping me striving to become that person? Loads of ordinary people just like me get there, so why the hell can't I?"

Then, for every dream that excites you, ask yourself why you want to become that person in that image you have just painted.

Somewhere in this process, I feel sure you will find a purpose that excites you, that has meaning for you. Something that will make life richer for you and the people around you.

Don't worry if you don't find it straight away. Often, the thought pattern takes time to develop.

Play with a few ideas in your head.
Test them out by saying them out loud to yourself. See if they sound right.
Then test them out on people you meet. Do they still sound right?
Write them down. Do they look right?
Select the one that is working for you. The one that feels right.
Sit on it and go back to it after a week, a month. Then again in another month. Is it still feeling good? Is it standing the test of time?
Are you starting to enjoy saying it to yourself and others?
Begin the first steps of acting on your purpose. Does it feel right?
Are you now saying it naturally and with conviction?

Words and intentions start to come without any special effort, any special thought.

Now you are arriving at the place where your purpose is becoming established and set.

You now start behaving consistently in a way that is congruent with your purpose and your journey has begun.

This process for some can take months or even years.
For some, it is very quick.

For some, they have always known it inside but don't know how to start on the journey, so it just sits there as a dormant force waiting to be unlocked.

For most, it can be found if you go and look for it hard enough.

A purpose can, and often does evolve with time. A purpose that takes you successfully through one phase of your life can become obsolete and be replaced with another that can serve to take you to another level or in another direction.

For this reason, it's not wise to seek absolute perfection in refining your purpose before starting on the journey. If your purpose feels substantially right and is giving you the internal drive and energy to move forward, then go with it. Evolution happens faster when there is action and momentum. Don't use the 'seeking perfection' thought as an excuse for inaction. You will never get there if you don't begin!

Finding your purpose exercise

Dreams I have had of who I could be. Dreams of what I could achieve.	Why is this important to me?
1	
2	
3	
4	
5	
6	

Building your future identity

Now we might be starting to form some ideas on why we are embarking on this journey. The next step is to design your future self.

If you get nothing else from this book, I really hope this section resonates with you, as I believe it is the single most important part of making quantum leaps in your performance and achievement.

Once you are able to paint a picture of what you want to become, then the next step is to 'fast forward' yourself into that person right now in the way you think of yourself.

So, if you want to be the owner of a market-leading £5 million tech company, then think and act as a successful tech entrepreneur NOW.

If you want to be a successful YouTube Channel owner, then think and act like one NOW.

If you want to be an Olympian, think and act as an Olympian NOW.

If you tell yourself an identity story consistently, things just start to happen that support this narrative. Step by step you get progressively closer to becoming this person in reality.

I would understand if at this point you are skeptical of this idea or maybe totally disbelieving. However, this happens not through any voodoo magic, but through something that is physiologically happening in your brain.

The Reticular Activating System (RAS) is a bundle of nerves at our brainstem that filters out unnecessary information so that the important stuff gets through. It's a valve (or filter) in your brain that decides what is allowed through from to your conscious thought from your sub-conscious thought.

Your brain is getting millions of sub-conscious messages constantly, far more than your conscious brain can process. Your RAS only lets through what it thinks is relevant, based on what you told it is relevant.

Let me give you an example:

You are having a mundane day at work and after a chat with a workmate you decide that you need (want) a new car. After chatting through a few ideas, you come to fancy the idea of buying a new A-Class Mercedes in metallic silver. You drive home along the M4. What do see? Yes, lots of A-Class Mercedes; in all colours but you really notice the silver ones. Yesterday on exactly the same journey you did not see ANY A-Class Mercedes at all.

What happened? Quite simply, you told your RAS to pull A-Class Mercedes into your conscious thoughts. They are now part of the relevant data set that is allowed through the RAS filter.

This same thing happens with my clients all of the time.

I worked with a great designer who wanted to grow his business. His self-identity was as a designer so he was not tuned in to all the things a business owner needs to think about. We worked hard to move his identity to one of being the owner of a £20 million creative company. It took a while to make the shift, but when it came it fundamentally changed his behaviour. He started to see new commercial opportunities and meet business partners that he just would not have seen and met in his old identity as a designer. His RAS was re-set to owning a large creative business and that is exactly what transpired.

I worked with a great teacher. She had a teaching business that matched tutors to parents who wanted to give their children tuition at home. She was very passionate about teaching and the benefits this bought to the children, the teachers and the parents. The web-based matching system was starting to show signs of fast growth and I knew she needed a different identity to capture the incredible potential of her idea. We worked on her identity as being a tech entrepreneur rather than a teacher. When the shift happened, her RAS successfully re-set, and she rose to the new challenge magnificently. She invested in tech infrastructure, digital marketing and built a support team in a matter of months. I am 100% certain she will go on and fulfill her potential.

This RAS re-set also changes your behaviour and body language. If the mind is fast-forwarding to a future, you then start to behave in this manner too. You can suddenly hold a credible conversation with a potential investor, with future business partners. You are constantly thinking through new technical ideas, researching and learning from others.

The fact is that an idea so fanciful as 'just think that you are already a superhero and you are very likely to become one' happens to be to absolutely true. This is quite incredible. However, I have witnessed it over and over again and it always fills me with sheer wonderment about the incredible power of the human brain.

Of course, it takes more than just the RAS being set in the right place to achieve the numerous milestones on your journey. All the elements within the three pillars need to come together to do this. However, without your ability to self-set your RAS to a future identity, you cannot get there.

Tips on RAS setting

A practical way of re-setting your RAS is to develop a set of 'I AM' statements. You can do this for every component of your life that forms the complete future you:

In your role as a father, mother, son, daughter, husband, wife, brother, sister, friend, mentor etc.
As a sportsman, orator, writer, businessman, politician, doctor, lawyer, artist, musician, etc
As a philanthropist, pioneer, thinker, prophet, influencer, etc.
As a leader, entrepreneur, investor, business guru, etc.

A few examples:

I am a loving and generous brother to my two sisters.
I am a role model to my grandchildren.
I am an inspirational leader to my team.
I am a successful entrepreneur.
I am a sought-after speaker and renowned expert on British politics.

I am a pioneer in the field of data science.

I am the best right winger in English rugby.

Once you have these, then it's just a case of practising this narrative over and over again in your head. At first, it sounds really stupid to you. It certainly did for me! (I did it when nobody else was around at first, in case anyone got wind of what I was doing and thought I had lost the plot!). However, this soon wears off as the first small shoots of progress start to emerge.

Another powerful mechanism of locking in your new identity is to share it publicly. Then there is no going back.

Mohammed Ali was probably the most accomplished at this. Very early in his career he told the world he was 'the greatest'. His RAS was now firmly fixed by virtue of the fact that he had committed to millions of his fans that he would fulfill this role. Everything he thought and did was congruent with this identity. He did what he needed to do make it a reality.

Jose Mourinho did a similar thing when he arrived at Chelsea FC. Whilst this was a big career jump, he told the press he was 'the special one' from the very start. Just like Ali, his identity was fixed and he rose to fulfill the role that he had created for himself. Chelsea became the most successful team in the English Premier League under his reign.

So why not experiment with making a public commitment on one of your 'I AM' statements.

The other part of establishing your aspirant identity is creating the right environment around you that re-enforces the new narrative.

If you want to become an Olympian then join a sports club that has athletes who are Olympians, or that has athletes with a similar aspiration as you. Put yourself in an environment that supports your identity and keeps your RAS firmly fixed in the right place. If this is a step too far, then join a club that is a feeder club to the one you really want to join.

This applies to the peer group of people you mix with. You may need some new friends who live and work in the space you want to be in. So, if you want to be a YouTube channel owner, then join a forum where other successful channel owners hang out.

Whilst this might sound scary at first, think back to the peer groups you have been in so far in your life. After a while in any peer group you always find a position in the group which is at least on a par with the average of that peer group. You naturally learn how to keep up with the pace of the group if you want to stay in it. So choosing the right peer group is a pretty important decision.

Seemingly small things can make a big difference to how you feel about yourself. What you are wearing, how you are travelling, what you are driving. Does the overall picture of your future self all hang together and help support your RAS?

Think also about how you introduce yourself to others.
When someone asks you what you do, what do you reply?
There is a big difference between:
I run a teaching organisation and *I own a fast-growth tech company in the education space.*
I am a rower and *I am training to row for the GB Team in the Tokyo Olympics.*

These introductions not only set your RAS, but also start committing you to take up your new role, both pulling and pushing you along the path.

So now it's your turn to define your Identity:

Role (ie Vocation, Mother, Brother etc.)	Identity
	I am
	I am
	I am
	I am
	I am

What changes in your environment do you need to make to grow into your identity?

The winning mindset

Life rewards those who approach it with the best mindset.

It does not yield its gifts automatically. It does so as a result of you constantly asking questions of it, and then it gradually reveals its limitless treasures.

In other words, the way you think about life is perhaps the most important factor in how life treats you.

Just like the way you measure the financial health of a business by its P and L (Profit and Loss), I look at how healthy we are thinking in terms of a mindset P and L.

The mindset P and L stands for:

Positive   and   Learning Rate
Proactive
Progressive

The Mindset P and L recognises that to grow you have to operate outside your comfort zone. In this space, you are going to make multiple errors (which is an uncomfortable activity for us). However, we have learnt that it's how you respond to the mistakes and setbacks that dictates the success you achieve, not how you deal with the things that go right.

High performers are constantly trying new things that often go wrong. This is the natural way humans learn. For example, if you watch a baby playing, what is it actually doing? It tries multiple ways of producing an outcome until it finds an outcome it likes. Then it repeats this task over and over again until it masters it. Just because we are older it does not mean this natural learning mechanism is any less effective!

As adults our appetite for experimentation tends to decrease because we get less good at dealing with the emotional side of the multiple attempts that don't work. Society starts to label these outcomes as failure rather than another step to finding the right answer. We all hate the idea of failure, so we learn habits to avoid the failure label.

We learn how to **dodge mistakes** so they do not get associated with us and hence we don't have to deal with the **perceived** negative consequences.

We become masters of devising amazing excuses.
It was going to snow where I live, so I am not going across to meet the customer.
I am not training tonight as my sister has a cold.
We lost the sale because the customer fancied the salesman from our competition.

We learn how to adeptly apportion blame to other people or things.
If you guys had stayed focussed we would not have let in three goals.
There are not many good people around so we can't recruit.
Our sales are poor because the market is difficult.

We learn how to play down the importance of the issue, in the hope it will go away. We deny a mistake has been made at all, even though it clearly has.
Our customers will still keep buying even though our satisfaction scores look poor.
I am still just as fit even though I might look overweight.
The new technology our competitors have looks good but ours is more reliable.

The better we get at this set of 'dodge it' habits, the worse our performance becomes. We learn how to avoid taking the actions needed to quickly get back on track. Instead we waste massive amounts of time and energy indulging in the art of dodge. If it were not such a waste of human energy it would be funny.

If I asked you to write down some of the best excuses you have heard, I bet you could come up with an impressive list. Each one was carefully thought about and crafted. You will certainly have a chuckle to yourself as you reflect on your list.

If I asked you to write down some the best excuses you have given yourself, how long would that be?

This list might not be quite so amusing, however.

In any situation if you allow yourself to indulge in this behaviour it just delays the inevitable action required *to do something positive about it,* and in the process sucks all the energy out of you and damages relationships with everyone involved. It's just a stupid ritual dance that we feel we need to go through in advance of getting on with things.

How many times have you spent more time discussing why something went wrong, who was to blame and was it really that bad after all rather than actually devising and implementing the solution.

The opposite reaction to mistakes and obstacles is P behaviour.

Positive. The attitude that immediately identifies the situation as an opportunity to learn something and a great challenge to overcome. It activates a trigger that energises your brain and body to engage in the issue immediately, to create a positive outcome for everyone involved. Obstacles and mistakes are sources of fun and fulfilment for P people. Often, if there aren't many obstacles to play with, P people create them just for the sheer satisfaction of solving them and learning something new.

Proactive. The attitude that actively looks for obstacles and seeks out challenges. They are opportunities in the mind of P people. Their brains have been trained to actively look for signs of things going astray so they can deal with them quickly to avoid them getting any worse (unlike the dodgers who try **not** to notice the warning signs and wait until the issue gets much bigger and harder to handle in the deluded hope that the issue might just disappear if they choose not see it).

Progressive. This is the forward-looking attitude, by engaging immediately in the actions that need to happen now and in the future, and not dwelling on what has happened in the past. P people know that they cannot impact anything that has already happened; they can only impact the present and the future, so this is where they spend their thoughts and energy. They also understand that there are many things that they just cannot control so they do not worry at all about these things, as they cannot impact them. They focus all their energy of solving the issue and extracting the maximum amount of learning from the occurrence and how it was overcome.

When I teach this to people everyone relates to it, and everyone has the absolute intention to get rid of their **dodge it** habits and immediately become a devout P person.

However, the Dodge it habits are perfectly natural, well ingrained and become more acute in higher pressure or stressful situations. So, living in the P zone, and avoiding D behaviour is not easy.

The trick is in the **language** we use with others and ourselves.

Firstly, when you come across an obstacle be mindful of what questions you immediately ask yourself and others.

If you ask **Why** something has happened, it triggers an inquest. The natural emotional response to this is the search for an **excuse** to offer. So, by using the Why question we are thrown quickly into dodge behaviour without intentionally meaning to drop into this zone.

If you ask **Who** has done something, it also triggers an inquest. The natural emotional response is the search for someone to assign **blame** to. So again, we can very quickly be thrown in the energy-sapping and unproductive world of dodge behaviour without realising what is going on. This happens very quickly and totally unintentionally.

However, if you train yourself to start with a **What** question, it triggers the brain to look for options to resolve the issue.

i.e. 'What can we do to solve this issue as fast as possible?'

The emotional response to this is both creative and collaborative and immediately raises the response into the P zone. You and others around you stay in the present and future. 'What can we do right now to resolve the issue and get back on track?'

To create this P culture around you, you have to neutralise the Why and Who questions quickly.

P people do this in a few different ways.

- They immediately assume personal ownership of the situation. They use the words "I" and "my" immediately. They avoid "you" or "they". Their attitude is: 'This is my problem, so let's find a way to solve it'. This puts everyone directly in the P zone as the need to search for any excuses has just evaporated.

- They accept accountability for the issue and are prepared to show vulnerability. 'This was my fault, I accept full accountability'. Again, this catapults everyone into the P zone because the need to find someone to blame has immediately gone. They don't care that this could make them vulnerable to criticism.

  They have strong self-belief and value the outcome more than the risk of the being criticized by others. They understand also that people probably know the reality and come to admire people who take accountability even if the fault did not lie directly with them.

- They don't allow it to become personal by using personal language. So, if they see someone slipping into the D zone they use neutral, never personal language.

For example, they would say...'Hey Jack let's stay in P zone here.' They would never say, 'Jack, are you blaming Fred for this?' They understand that good and fast decision-making relies on keeping everyone cool-headed and un-emotional. Personal language just makes people emotional and is totally counterproductive.

Neutral language can be developed by teaching the people around you a model that describes both positive and negative behaviour in easy-to-remember phrases.

I use the Mindset P&L as my neutral language.

Others use 'Above and below the line' as their neutral language to explain the key behaviours.

You can adopt one of these, or create your own.

P Zone Positive response Proactive response Progressive response	P Language **What** can we do now to resolve and learn? **How** can we get this fixed as fast as possible?	*Winning Mindset* ↑
D Zone Dodge it with an excuse. Dodge it by blaming others. Dodge it by denying there is an issue.	D Language **Why** did this happen? **Who** was responsible for this?	*Victim Mindset* ↓

The L in mindset P and L is all about learning to learn.

The rate of progression along your chosen path is, to a large extent, governed by the rate at which you can learn. The faster you learn, the faster you grow. In a competitive situation, the trick is to learn faster than your next best competitor.

So, it makes sense to perfect our personal technique of learning.

We have covered the attitude required to learn in the P section. However, there is more to the learning mindset.

Time – How much time do you dedicate to learning?

If you want to learn about a subject, then you have to plan time in your schedule to learn. The clients I work with plan in time for reading, listening and watching material on specific subjects they want to learn about. They go to seminars and visit people who are sharing information about these subjects.

The key to this is the focused nature of the learning. If you really want to learn something for a specific reason then it's easy to dedicate quality time to this activity.

I was never interested in foreign languages so never did well at school in these subjects. My teachers told me I had neither the aptitude nor attitude for foreign languages. When I accepted a job based in Spain in my mid-twenties, I learnt how to speak Spanish and accomplished a good level of fluency in less than two years. I found the focus and motivation to learn.

The mindset of learning is that it's just another part of your vocation and you plan it in the same way. If you only participate in learning activities 'in your spare time', then your learning rate will be far too slow for this journey.

The L mindset proactively has a constant learning plan.

Making new mistakes?

> *"Success is the ability to go from one failure to*
> *another with no loss of enthusiasm."*
> – Winston Churchill

The rate at which you make mistakes dictates the rate at which you learn. Depending on how fast you want to learn, or how fast you need to learn, you can choose how fast you want to make mistakes. If you are in a field that requires lots of innovation, lots of new knowledge, then you need to make mistakes fast because you need to learn fast. In this situation, there is no other source of learning apart from your self-generated knowledge. A planned programme of experimentation is required.

The rate of making mistakes is also dependent on your attitude towards risk. The more supportive of risk-taking you are, the more new mistakes are 'allowed' to happen and the higher the rate of learning.

A tech company I was recently working with realized they had to develop their software product much faster than their competition. They developed a policy of actively encouraging their team members to make as many **'new mistakes'** as possible every week. In their weekly team meetings, each team member shared the new mistakes they had made each week. Using the language of new mistakes and the supportive structure, they were able to develop new software products at a very fast pace. The process of team members freely trying things that they did not know how to do, discarding what did not work but discovering quickly what did work, drove their development programme.

In other areas in which knowledge already exists, and growth involves acquiring that knowledge as fast as possible, then this level of risk-taking is not required or necessary.

As you embark on your journey, set your compass based on the rate and type of learning you will need to accomplish. Accept the appropriate level of associated risk and build your mindset around these settings.

Learning by seeking and responding to feedback

Learning is greatly accelerated by the process of receiving feedback from people who really care about you and your journey.

All of us have blind spots. We have an internal view of our performance which sometimes correlates to a more objective view of reality and sometimes does not. In order to understand where we are reaching high standards and where we still need to improve and learn more, we need another pair of eyes to see what we cannot see.

As a coach I play this role for my clients, and I employ someone else to play this role for me. I have learnt the positive impact that regular and honest feedback has on my performance.

As an example, I was recently a speaker at a conference of other coaches from around the UK. When I came off stage I was very happy with my performance across most dimensions that I was attempting to achieve. Luckily, the conference organizer had asked the audience to rate my performance. I read each and every feedback form. I quickly understood that my performance had resonated really well for certain types of people in the audience (people who were similar to me). However, different types of people needed more detail and examples behind some of the themes I was presenting. I would never have understood this without this quality and quantity of feedback and would certainly have made the same mistake again. This feedback was really valuable in helping me learn fast.

When I was younger, I struggled with feedback. I have always been passionate about my work and tended to take feedback very personally. I had the wrong mindset and, frankly, I was not emotionally mature enough to re-set it. This really held me back as, naturally, people became reluctant to offer feedback freely as they were cautious of the emotional reaction they might get.

I recently did some work with a member of the British Olympic rowing team who really explained beautifully how feedback fits into the mindset of high performance. He explained that you needed to become a 'good psychopath' to improve and perform in high-pressure situations. What he meant was that that you have to utilize a switch in your brain to turn off emotions when receiving feedback or performing under pressure, otherwise your brain cannot process the new information in the cold and calculating way needed to make objective decisions. So, after a training session or approaching a race he put his mind into a calm, emotionless state. A state that he had practised many times. In this state, he was able to process information effectively and make rational decisions based on the learnt codes that his training had taught him.

It's this skill that makes the highly trained SAS troops so effective in combat situations.

So the L mindset is firstly to learn how to accept feedback in a non-emotional manner, and build the new information into your performance habits as a mechanism for constant incremental improvement.

The L mindset also sets up feedback mechanisms to get the quantity and quality of feedback required.

High performers hire mentors, trainers and coaches to give them a regular stream of objective feedback which is the fuel that drives their learning momentum.

Learning by finding your limits.

My PT asked me the other day how many sit-ups I can do.

'No idea,' I responded.

'Guess,' he said.

'I think I could push to 50,' I responded optimistically.

'Ok, let's try... keep going until you can't do any more.'

I was not so enthusiastic about this idea as we were already 40 minutes into a rigorous work-out, but I went for it nevertheless.

I got to 40 and started hurting. I pushed on to 50 and pain was there but not getting worse. At 60, I felt like I was close to failure. At 75, I could not physically squeeze out another one regardless of how much he told me that I could do another 5.

As I lay on the mat (unable to get up) it struck me that I had just learnt something important about myself. My limit was 75 not 50. So, exercising at below 50 was a self-limiting thought.

How many other areas of my life was I operating below my capacity? Did I even understand my capacity?

After this thought, I talked to a number of people about this idea and discovered that high performers often push themselves to the point of failure to find their limits.

Not just in sport but in many other areas.

For example:

- *You will not know what price you get for your product if you don't price it higher.*
- *You will never know how many miles you could cycle off-road in one day if you don't start at 6am one day and cycle until you drop.*
- *You will never know how many great employees you can attract if you don't market the opportunity as hard as you can.*
- *You will never know how much money you could raise for your new venture unless you ask for much more than you think you need.*

The mindset behind this is one than does not accept a perceived limit. The limit to anything is the maximum that can be achieved by actually testing the limit.

In sport, for instance, you only train up to a percentage of what you believe your limit is.

However, if one day your coach pushes you beyond your perceived limit to a place you would never have gone alone, then your new limit has moved and you start training closer to this new limit. You have moved up to the next level.

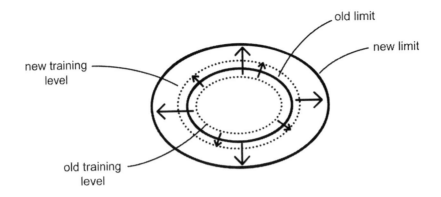

old limit

new limit

new training level

old training level

It is this mindset that forces learning.

The moment I had achieved my 75 sit-ups, my mind went directly to active questioning, 'What could I do differently or better to get to 80? What if I adjusted my position? What if I focused my gaze on a single point on the wall? What if I totally distracted my thoughts on something else to mask the pain?'

These were thoughts that I would just not have generated if I had done my normal 2 sets of 40.

So L players think big in order to find their limits. They don't ask what would be a good result. They ask: what is the maximum result possible? Then they test the limit and measure the result. Then, they change one thing and see what happens. They learn something that helps them get to the next level.

It is only by focusing on this constant incremental improvement that you can get to find exceptional performance in the areas you choose to play. It's a constant, never-ending learning process.

Energy for Life

You know how it feels sometimes when you are really in the flow of things. You feel in control of what you are doing, you feel confident and your thinking is clear and focused. You are performing well and life feels good. You have boundless energy and feel like you could go on forever.

Then something knocks you out of this zone, normally an emotional reaction to something or someone.

You question if what you are doing is right, you get annoyed about a colleague or employee, you don't feel so good, you lose your sense of organisation and your to-do list is getting longer and longer, etc.

You are now out of the performance zone and life feels like a struggle again. Your energy levels drop.

One the biggest differences between those who achieve great things and those who do not is the ability to stay in the performance zone for the maximum amount of time. If you think about it, your output is going to be directly proportional to the time spent in this zone. The longer you are in it, the more you are going to achieve.

So, this section is about learning how to stay in the performance zone for as long as possible. I am not proposing that it's possible to stay there permanently as this would be super-human. Maybe one day they will invent robots that can do this, but for the purpose of this book let's assume we are all 'normal' humans.

The Performance Zone

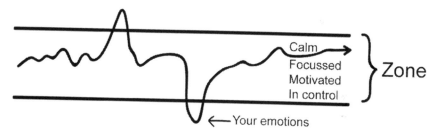

To stay in the performance zone, we have to learn to control our emotions, as it is purely our emotions that are going to knock us out. Our emotions are triggered by our thoughts, so in fact it's the control of our thinking that is the real challenge we are attempting to master.

This is a constant challenge for all of us, a challenge that gets harder the more you challenge yourself to perform at a higher level. As you challenge yourself, you put yourself into a high-performance environment and staying in the zone becomes ever more difficult.

I spent a while last summer talking to one of the coaches of the GB rowing team on this subject. She told me that once you get plunged into this high-performance environment you have no choice but to learn the techniques to keep your mind and body in the zone. It's sink or swim time. These athletes go through extreme training for months and years to compete in just a few races of just 4 minutes in duration, the result of which define their achievement and identity. They put their lives 'on hold' in the pursuit of achieving something very special. Approaching these major events, they need to stay firmly in the performance zone in order to compete at the highest level of their sport.

She explained that firstly you have to accept that you are in a high-performance environment and the day-to-day pressures within this environment are going to be extreme. Accept it and learn how to deal with it.

This was the first big lesson I took. If you want to find the best you can be, you are voluntarily putting yourself in a high-performance environment. In this environment it's going to feel pressured, it's going to feel uncomfortable at times. You will be out of your comfort zone for long periods of time.

This is your choice, so never complain about it. Accept it and learn how to manage it. It is not going to go away or even get any easier. Once you have mentally accepted this, it's much easier to deal with it.

In this environment, the pressure creates forces that pull your emotions all over the place, create such turbulence that you need other equal and opposite forces to keep you *in balance.*

She used the great analogy of the washing machine. In a high-performance environment it can feel like you are going around inside the drum. The vibration can topple the machine over if it is not tethered down with anchor ropes.

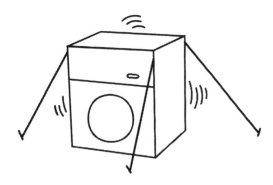

She went on to explain that everyone has their own set of anchors and, provided these anchors remain strong, she is able to keep her athletes stable and in the performance zone. The consequence of this is that people need to really understand their own anchors and work as hard on these as they do on the core focus of their vocation.

If you lose an anchor then it's important you recognise this and replace it with another or get it fixed before your 'washing machine' topples over.

I can certainly recognise this in myself. When reflecting on what she had said I was able to identify my anchors immediately.

These are:

- Relationships. (My relationship with my wife and children needs to be in good shape for me to feel balanced.)
- Exercise. (I need to be exercising 3 to 4 times a week for me feel balanced.)
- Eating and drinking. (I need to eat and drink well, avoid excesses of fried food and alcohol for me to feel balanced.)
- Learning. (I need to be engaged in some type of learning activity all of the time for me to feel balanced.)
- Recovery time. (I like to work hard, but I need regular and good quality recovery time to feel balanced.)
- Fun. (I need a good laugh and a joke pretty regularly for me to feel balanced.)

When I am not in flow and life feels like a struggle, it's normally a result of one or more of these things not working for me. My thoughts get out of control and my emotions drag me out of my performance zone in the areas of my life that I really want to perform well at.

The other thing that a washing machine has is a pause button. Sometimes you just need to stop the machine. Take a period of reflection to understand better what you are doing. Adjust a few things. Refresh your energy before hitting the on button again.

This realisation has really helped me give these anchors more attention. I am mindful of my need to schedule time and energy into these areas every week, as I now know the effect of not looking after my anchors. Whilst I used to consider these things as indulgences I now consider them as fundamentals that rank equally alongside anything else that I give focus to in the week.

I also learned that I needed to get better at some of these areas to strengthen the anchor.

On the exercise front, I hired a Personal Trainer – not to teach me how to train but to give me the regular accountability and discipline to exercise. He is tough on me in the one session we do together every week and if I don't exercise in between I know it's really going to hurt! I also don't mind paying him well and up-front because I know that I am not going to be tempted to miss sessions I have paid for. These are simple triggers I have created for myself to make it easy for me to do what I want to do, rather than relying on hard self-discipline alone. Rationally, I know that I could exercise just as well and just as regularly without paying a Personal Trainer, but emotionally I know that creating triggers and accountability will massively increase the probability that I will actually do it.

On the learning side, I always have one project on the go, sometimes more. Projects require focused learning in order to produce an outcome. These range from building a house to writing a book. Whatever it is, I now realise that it's not the outcome that is important, but the learning that is required to create that outcome. My crazy projects (as termed by my family) create the trigger I need for my learning anchor. I used to think that I may indeed be a little crazy, but now I understand that I need this in my life to remain balanced and provide the focus I need in the more important areas of my life in which I want to perform at a high level. I now understand that the projects themselves don't necessarily have to be successful, providing that the learning involved was fulfilling for me. I have loved writing this book, for example. It was a great project that in itself has sustained one of my anchors in good shape for many months.

For every anchor to remain strong, we all need to have triggers that help us build and maintain the required habits.

Often, we also need others around us to help us: to give us a trigger to act, to give us some accountability to do what we said we wanted to do rather than just take the easy option.

So, what are your anchors?
What are your triggers?
What are the things that will help you create and maintain the strength of each anchor?
Who do you need around you to trigger action and keep you accountable?

My Anchors

1)	
2)	
3)	
4)	
5)	
6)	

For each anchor, describe how it needs to be to give it strength, the triggers you could use to maintain it and the people you could use to provide the triggers and some accountability.

Anchor 1:
This anchor is strong when I:
The triggers I can use to make it easy are:
The people I can use to give me the triggers and hold me accountable:

Anchor 2:
This anchor is strong when I:
The triggers I can use to make it easy are:
The people I can use to give me the triggers and hold me accountable:

Anchor 3:
This anchor is strong when I:
The triggers I can use to make it easy are:
The people I can use to give me the triggers and hold me accountable:

Anchor 4:

This anchor is strong when I:

The triggers I can use to make it easy are:

The people I can use to give me the triggers and hold me accountable:

Anchor 5:

This anchor is strong when I:

The triggers I can use to make it easy are:

The people I can use to give me the triggers and hold me accountable:

Anchor 6:

This anchor is strong when I:

The triggers I can use to make it easy are:

The people I can use to give me the triggers and hold me accountable:

The three core anchors

For some people, exercise and healthy, nutritious food are anchors for different reasons than to keep their body and mind in good shape.

Exercise, for instance, releases chemicals called **endorphins,** which make you feel good. It is also good 'me time' which gives you space to think.

The act of eating good food with others provides the social glue that builds relationships, fun and enjoyment.

However, to perform at our best we know we need to keep our bodies in good shape.

There are only two things you need to master in this respect:

Good nutrition and regular exercise

These sound really basic. However, I meet people every day that are under-performing because they are not actively managing the maintenance of their bodies. After all, you only have one of them and it does not last forever. The better you maintain it, the better it will perform and the longer it will last.

Just like the other elements of the four pillars, learning some good habits in this area will give you a massive payback on the effort it takes upfront.

If nothing else, it gives you more energy for life. The more energy you have, the more you do; the more experiences you have, the more life you live.

Nutrition

Everyone is different and everyone requires different nutrition in different phases of their lives.

There is little doubt that what you eat and when you eat it is a major factor in how you feel, the energy levels you have, the stamina you have and your overall capacity to perform.

But how many of us actually know what their optimum nutrition pattern is?

How many of us get expert advice on how to eat a diet that is both enjoyable and sets up your body for optimal performance?

High performers in all walks of life take this seriously, just as elite athletes do.

They not only **learn** from experts what diet works for their body but also have the **discipline** to follow it.

So, the best option is to find a nutritionist to help you. They are not expensive and there are lots of them around. Ask for referrals from your GP and your Personal Trainer.

The other option is just to 'listen' to our bodies. Most of us know our bodies pretty well, but just don't prioritise what they are telling us above other things that we decide are more important.

For example, our eating pattern might be:

Rushing out of the door in the morning and grabbing a piece of toast on the way. This is not going to set you up for the key activities you want to perform well at during the morning. Even if you have time, if the only thing you have in the cupboard is coco pops and coffee, then you are doomed to a poor morning.

High performers plan their mornings really well, as it's actually the only time of the day that is truly yours to control. If you get up before the phone starts to ring or the kids arrive downstairs for breakfast, you have some quality time that is 100% yours. Getting up a bit earlier and eating a good nutritious breakfast in a calm atmosphere sets you up for the day. If you start well, often the rest of the day follows suit.

Eating at regular intervals during the day is also important for most of us. It maintains your energy levels and the eating breaks keep your ability to concentrate high. But if we prioritise rushing to another meeting, or thrashing through more emails over taking an eating break, then we are accepting that paradigm that somehow looking after yourself comes after all those 'work' tasks: the crazy paradigm that you only take time to look after yourself if you 'have time after work'.

If you can reverse this paradigm to one of 'it's fundamental to eat and drink well, so I can perform at my best in everything I do throughout the day,' then your performance will improve.

To make this habit easy, then put more time into planning your shopping well. Schedule it in your calendar. If you have a stock of great quality food and drink around you during the day, then it's easy to eat well. If these are not to hand, we often just don't eat at the right time or we buy from the nearest convenient place. This convenience food culture that we are migrating towards is tough on our bodies as it relies on being close to places that sell high-quality tasty food in the time and place that you are hungry. The somewhat random nature of this means that we only end up eating well on a small proportion of the meals we eat. Why not fit cupboards and fridges into your workplace and keep them stocked with the right type of high-quality foods? Keep you and the people around you in good shape.

Eating well for most of us does require more effort for the simple reason that pre-prepared and processed foods are mostly laden with a whole load of sugars, fats, pesticides, etc. that are just not good for our bodies.

So, unless you are lucky enough to have a personal chef, then buying and preparing food from fresh is a key part of eating well. The good habit here, however, is not so much about taking the time to cook, but taking the time to plan the meals for the week and making sure you have the right ingredients in to make the right meal. If you have great ingredients available to you, it really does not take much effort to prepare great food that is tasty and enjoyable to eat.

There is a perception that healthy food is more expensive. Personally, I don't think that is the case… but even if it was, then it still has to be a great investment. You will perform better by eating better food, so you will earn more to pay for it.

Would you buy a Ferrari then fill it with cheap oil so it can't perform to its full potential?

Exercise

The human body needs regular exercise to maintain itself. It's a finely-tuned machine that can only perform if properly maintained.

Exercise has multiple benefits above that of core maintenance. It reduces stress and anxiety and it puts the mind in a reflective (thinking mode). How many great ideas have you had when out on a run or on a treadmill?

When you feel fit, your self-esteem is improved and your mental toughness is optimized.

To operate in a high-performance environment, these attributes are essential tools to navigating the many obstacles and challenges that we encounter along the way.

So, finding an exercise regime that works for you is essential.

For most of us, a minimal requirement of 40 minutes of aerobic exercise 3 times per week is required.

Finding exercise habits that are both fun and easy is the key, as it's never a problem starting a new activity, the problem comes in maintaining it.

In the section on anchors, we talked about triggers and having someone to hold you accountable. The area of exercise is probably the area that most us find the most need for this.

There are lots of ways of making exercise easy and fun:

- Pick a sport that is fun.

- Find activities that other people you like to spend time with also like.
- Dance!
- Build a gym in your house.
- Sign up to a video work-out programme with charismatic trainers like Shaun T or Joe Wicks.

I had a client who was struggling to get in sync with a regular exercise programme. I suggested that he buy some fitness equipment and exercise before he goes to work. He was a busy entrepreneur and struggled to find any space in his schedule during the day or evening. He also loved his gadgets and confidently told me he had a top-of-the-range treadmill out in a building in the garden that they used as a gym. I asked him what was his favourite room in the house and suggested he moved the treadmill to this room and preferably position it right in front of a big TV screen. After a debate about the negotiation that he would need to have with his wife about moving the machine into their family room, he agreed to give it a go. I totally forgot about the conversation for a couple of months, but one day commented on how well he looked. He smiled and said that since he moved the treadmill, he had managed to exercise several times a week. 'It's just so easy to jump out of bed, switch on the TV to the morning news programme and jump on the treadmill for 25 minutes,' he said. Making it easy and fun to exercise by this simple move of a piece of equipment 10 meters from one room to another enabled him to find a habit he liked. He became a high performer and built a really exciting company and a beautiful family over the following years. He found a better version of himself.

If you have not included exercise and nutrition in your anchor plan, then look at this area again.

Rest and Recovery

The third core anchor is rest and recovery. High levels of performance can only be sustained if you allow enough time between activities to properly rest and recover. Everyone's minds and bodies are different, so recovery periods do vary. The important thing, however, is to recognise the value and necessity of planning in your recovery periods and putting yourself in the right environment and state of mind to recover effectively. These periods are equally as important as the activity itself.

This includes recovery time during the day, recovery during the week and recovery time during the year. I always encourage my clients to book their holiday weeks in advance and spread them evenly across the year. Holiday weeks are essential to get the deep rest you need to stay sharp during the year.

Part 1: The Self-Mastery Checklist

Now you know the areas it takes to master yourself, I have included the **Self-Mastery Checklist** so you can monitor your own performance in this area.

Self Mastery Checklist

Areas	Score (1-5) (1 = No, 5= Absolutely Yes)
Purpose Do I have clear a purpose ? Can I articulate it with passion and conviction ? Does it provide a strong enough force to pull me forward ? *Identity* Do I know who I want to be? Do I know the key roles I want to play in life? Do I have I AM statements for each role? Am I using my I AM statements to set my RAS? *Mindset* Do I consistently think and act in the P zone? Do I use P Language? Do I dedicate quality time to learning? Do I seek and embrace new mistakes? Do I have strong sources of feedback? Do I seek my limits? *Energy* Do I know my anchors? Are my anchors strong? Am I working to maintain/improve my anchors? Does my diet keep me healthy? Does my exercise routine keep me fit? Do I feel energized most of the time?	
Total	

PART TWO

CONNECTIVITY

Connectivity

We are all made to live in societies (or tribes) rather than alone.

It has always been so that those who achieve more, do so by attracting the support of others around them. They know that the scale of their achievement is in direct proportion to the amount of people they enlist to help them in pursuit of their goals.

They build alliances, teams, and collaborations to join forces with like-minded people and focus the combined energy and passion of these groups (tribes) to the achievement of feats that are infinitesimally greater that one could achieve by working alone.

This ability to *connect* with others is a core skill area that can be learned and is a significant success driver for high-performing people.

The great connectors develop what is often referred to as high levels of emotional intelligence (as opposed to IQ which is a measure of intellectual skills).

Emotional intelligence is in simple terms the ability to deeply understand the thoughts and emotions of others around them, and develop **behavioural and communication skills that influence and persuade people to help them in the pursuit of their goals.**

This set of skills can certainly be learnt and anyone can get significantly better at surrounding themselves with talented and like-minded people that will increase their rate of progression and achievement.

There are many skills in the field of developing emotional intelligence but for the purpose of connectivity I have broken it down to the four areas that are most critical to become competent in.

Understanding yourself and others.
The power of curiosity.
Influence and Attraction.
Communication.

Understanding People

The first person we need to understand is ourselves.

When we have a good understanding of ourselves it allows us to do three things:

- Fully utilise our natural strengths and use others to support us with those things that we are not naturally good at or just don't like doing.
- Learn to adapt our natural behaviours to connect better with people who have very different behavioural profiles to our own.
- Always be working on a personal development plan that helps us develop stronger behaviours that work better for both ourselves and the people around us.

We all have a natural behavioural profile: our default setting. This is a set of behaviours that is specific to us. When in a relaxed state and behaving naturally, it's this set of behaviours that we exhibit. We also tend to 'default' to this behaviour set when put under pressure or stress.

In between these two states, we have a 'learned' or 'adapted' behavioural template that we have created to better suit the demands of our day-to-day life.

Sometimes our 'natural' profile and our 'adapted' profile is almost identical. In this case, we either have a vocation that is perfectly suited to natural behavioural pattern or we are just so self-assured that we feel able to be ourselves in both roles.

If our natural and adapted profile is too far apart, then we may be finding that our vocation is hard work and often stressful, as we are working at a distance from our natural state. For much of our time we are able to do this, but the tensions can get quite acute when the pressure is on and we have to be really mindful not to revert to our default settings.

The good news is that as humans we have the ability to be chameleon-like in nature. If we are aware of the behavioural profile of our audience, we can quickly adopt their profile and connect with them much more quickly and effectively. Often people judge each other extremely quickly, so the ability to read someone and adapt is something that needs both knowledge and practice. This skill is a very powerful weapon in your connectivity armoury.

There are many profiling methods out there to help you understand the differing behavioural types. The top ones are all good and very similar in nature.

For the purpose of explaining the profile map, I will use the DISC system.

This categorizes the key behavioural traits into 4 categories.

D = Dominant
I = Influencing
S = Steady
C= Conscientious

Most of us have a mix of these traits in both our natural and adapted profiles. Some of us have one of these as an extreme type. I.e. People who are very high on the D category (Hi D's) are very recognizable as demonstrating the D behaviours. You can spot them easily.

Other people have an even mix of these characteristics and are much harder to read.

To find out what your profile is, why not go to beperformancecoaching.com and fill out the questionnaire.

The table below gives a brief summary of the behaviours of the four profile types.

Dominant Demanding Decisive Dramatic Dynamic	**Influencing** Interesting Inspiring Impressionable
Conscientious Competent Cautious Calculating Careful	**Steady** Supportive Stable Sensitive Shy

To start to understand this, it's useful to contrast the traits.

Firstly, on the left-hand side of the grid (D and C) are task-orientated people. What's important to them is getting things done. The D's like tasks done quickly – they are dynamic and impatient. The C's like tasks done correctly and accurately. It's all about the getting the detail right for them.

On the right-hand side of the grid (I and S) we have people-orientated types. What's important to them is the person rather than the task. The I's love to talk and be liked by others. ('I' is a very relevant word as it's all about them). For the S's you are the important one. They care about you, and want to get to know and trust you before giving much of themselves away or participating in activities with you.

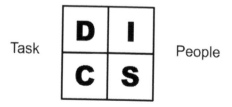

On the vertical axis, we have outgoing people on top of the grid (the D and I's). You notice these people in the group. The I's are attracting attention with their stories, jokes and anecdotes. The D's are directing the proceedings and being selective in who they interact with.

In the lower part of the grid, (the C's and S's) the people are reserved. The C's are normally 'in the kitchen at parties'. The S's are curious about others and often engage in long detailed conversations asking people all about their lives, without giving much away themselves. They tend to blend into the crowd.

Outgoing

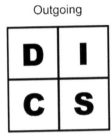

Reserved

I hope you are starting to form a picture. We start to recognize ourselves and others close to us.

Then we can observe what's important to each type.

For D's being powerful and a winner is very important. They love to compete, challenge and haggle. There is no fun in winning without being in a game in the first place! They often create games for the fun of creating competitive tension.

For C's being correct is important. They seek perfection. Things need to be in order, and right. They are uncomfortable if the i's are not dotted and the t's are not crossed. It's important that they are competent in what they do and they value competence in others.

For I's being liked is important. They are social animals that want to be accepted and popular in the tribe. They love recognition and hate to be ignored.

For S's harmony is important. They like the people around them to be getting on well. They value peace, hate conflict and become uncomfortable if their tribe is emotionally disjointed.

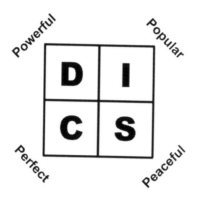

So how do you interact with a high D? Well, they are likely to challenge you up-front to see if you could be worth interacting with. If you are robust in your response and, better still, challenge back then you have their respect and attention. If you back off or show any sign of weakness, then they lose interest in you very fast. Once you have their attention you are not likely to have it for long as they are dynamic and decisive individuals who want to debate strongly, make a decision and move on. You will need to be concise and expressive in your approach to maintain a constructive connection.

For this reason, you have to plan your discussion in advance because you don't get long to get your point across.

It is always wise to ask them for much more than you need from the start, as they always attempt to negotiate a more favourable outcome for themselves. They need to feel like they have won, so best to be clear about what you need and start higher. It's also good to be clear about the line that you will not cross, so you can say no with conviction and speed if this arises.

When communicating in writing, they are likely to write very short sentences. Sometimes, just one word. They will not read long letters and emails from others. I learnt this when my wife had a client that was very high D. She got so frustrated with him because he either did not reply to her emails or he only dealt with one of the points she was trying to address. After a session on using DISC, she realised he was not being rude or ignorant but he was only reading either just the title or the first sentence of her emails. He was just programmed this way. My wife is a high I so her emails are naturally quite descriptive and polite. When she changed her writing style with him, communication became much better. She used much shorter notes with strong titles that summarised what was required. The important things she puts in bold. She now never puts multiple issues in one note but splits them up into separate notes, so he can reply using one word or one sentence. She has also cut out most of the personal greeting sentences, as she knows he is task focused and wants to get directly to the point. Her connectivity to this person has improved immensely since.

When interacting with a C orientated person then they share the task-orientated bias of the D's, however they do require the detail. They need to know exactly **what** is being proposed, **how** it is going to be done, **when** things are planned to happen and **how much** it is going to cost. If you attempt to 'blag' a C, then they recognise it immediately and lose respect for you. They view themselves as being competent and they only want to deal with other competent people.

I learnt this when I started recruiting clients for my coaching business. There was one person I remember distinctly as he was very precise about things in our initial discussion. As we ran out of time going through lots of detail, I agreed to ring him back one Friday afternoon. I phrased it that I would likely be back in the office around 2.30pm and I would call him then. In my mind, this meant any time from say 2.15 – 3.15 (I am pretty high on the I scale). I did not call him until just before 3pm and he gave me very short thrift. It was not until a few months afterwards when I got to know him socially that he explained that, at first, he did not think I was a very serious person as I failed to call him when I said I would. To him, being precise was important and he did not think he could work with me if I was 'loose' with timekeeping. That taught me a lesson. Since that day I have noted down the DISC profile of people and make sure I approach them in the appropriate manner.

This particularly applies to the I profile people. I know I need to leave lots of time for a phone call or meeting with this profile.

They will need to know that I like and appreciate them before we can do anything together, which means I will have to be in active listening mode for a fair bit of time. I say active listening because while listening to them express themselves I will need to respond positively to what they are saying without slowing them down or cramping their style. As my profile is high in I, this is particularly challenging for me as actually it's me who would prefer to be the one talking! I consciously have to tell myself to 'shut up' and be patient in these situations. I have learnt the art of asking questions and shutting up and listening. If you do this well then at least you can stay in control of the conversation whilst still allowing the person opposite to fully express themselves and feel that you are really interested in them by virtue of all the great questions you are asking them.

The key thing to remember here is that they are making a decision about you as a person more than the rational substance of the task or problem in hand. Once the mutual level of rapport is strong enough, then you can move on to discussing the issue in hand, but not before then. So, whilst they can be decisive, they are only so with people they really like and trust. In environments when they are making decisions for themselves, they are often indecisive and often change their minds. This is because they need to trust themselves in this environment which is often not so easy for people who trust emotional intelligence more than intellect.

The good thing with high I's is that they are naturally very open and trusting, so often this stage can be relatively quick. If you are a high I yourself, then be careful of this attribute as you tend to bestow trust before it has been truly earned, making you vulnerable to people who don't deserve your trust and subsequently don't fulfill your expectations of them.

Ongoing communication with I's follows this pattern. Greetings and 'banter' are an essential part of interacting successfully and you need to invest more time to connect well with this profile.

As they value the art of communication and practise it more than most, they tend to become very good at it and are capable of using these skills to influence others. This is why people who are involved in selling in any capacity tend to be strong in this profile. They enjoy the process of 'persuading' and 'influencing' others to buy through the art of communication.

Finally, we arrive at our S (Steady) people. This trait is also very people-oriented but for different reasons. Whilst the focus of I's is naturally themselves, the focus of S's is not themselves but the others around them. They want to know all about you before they can trust you enough to either give something of themselves away or interact with you in a meaningful manner.

They are not only concerned with knowing and trusting others but care about their wellbeing.

When interacting with an S then you will need to be prepared to talk and tell them all about yourself. Building strong relationships with them can often take a long time, but once built it is deep and secure. (Relationships with high I's are built much quicker, but are more superficial in the early days).

For this reason, decision making is a much slower process and you need to mindful of the realistic timeframe for things to happen when interacting with S's. They won't be rushed.

As harmony is important for S's then they tend to avoid conflict situations or environments where conflict is frequent. As a consequence of this trait, being mindful of how others will feel as a result of any change or decision is critical when interacting with this group.

They are the nurturers and team players. They treat people in a caring manner and expect to be treated this way in return.

How to use your new understanding of others.

Now that you have a mental map of how to plot differing types of people, and how to interact with them to improve your connectivity, let me add a few more tips.

The first is about identifying as quickly and accurately as possible the behavioural profile of the person you want to connect with.

In a critical situation like recruitment then of course you can ask them to complete a profile questionnaire and study the resultant report. This is a positive and enlightening exercise for both parties. It's also really important as job interviews are not 'natural' environments for people, so in true chameleon style the interviewee tries hard sub-consciously to adopt the style they think is most likely to connect with the interviewer. This can result in a disastrous mis-match between the type of person and the type of job. Imagine putting a high C into a sales role, or a high D into the role as a carer for the elderly or in a customer service role. No matter how much they like the idea of it, they are not going to be a natural fit.

How often have you been in a situation when the person you met at interview turns out to be a very different person a few weeks later when they removed their outer shell and started being their natural self? I know I have in my early career and these mistakes can be very stressful and expensive for both parties.

However, in most situations, you don't get the luxury of having a full DISC profile. You have to figure it out yourself by matching the behaviours you observe with the DISC map.

A good quick trick is to ask one killer question which most of the time reveals a person's dominant trait.

This question is simply: How are you today?

A person with a dominant D trait will answer with a definitive one-word reply such as Fine or Good. They are subconsciously telling you that they are not particularly interested in personal stuff and to get to the point of what you want to say.

A person with a dominant I profile will probably tell you the story of their day so far. "Well funny you should ask, I got up early today and tried those new multi-grain bars and I have to say I feel pretty good on it, etc etc etc." The point being it will be something more than just a simple reply, because they naturally want to express themselves and seek a positive response from you.

A person with a dominant S profile will probably respond by skipping over the question and asking how you are. "I'm ok but tell me, how are you?" They don't want to talk about themselves, but are genuinely interested in your wellbeing above their own.

A person with a dominant C profile will probably respond with sense of a double negative: "Not bad" or "Could be worse". They don't want to show undue enthusiasm for a day in which the outcome has not been defined yet.

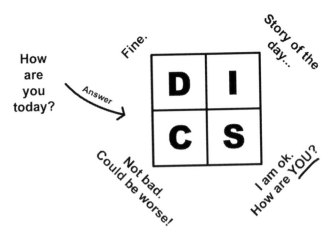

These simple responses are a great start to you becoming an expert connector.

When you can 'read' someone quickly and 'match and mirror' their natural behaviour, you can connect with them quickly and a relationship has commenced.

When you are mindful of someone's behavioural profile, you can adapt your style when interacting with them to stay well connected and to constantly build on the health and quality of all of the relationships that are important to you.

Exercise:

Part 1 – Self profile

Send an email to profiles@beperformancecoaching.com to get your own DISC profile.

Then ask yourself:

How do I leverage my natural dominant traits?

How do I compensate for the traits that are not in my profile but are important to parts of my life?

Given my profile, what type of people would it be useful to have around me?

What would be perfect roles for me?

Part 2 – Profiling Others

Pick 6 people that you interact with on a regular basis.

For each person figure out what their DISC profile is and ask yourself how you could more effectively interact with them as a result of this insight.

The power of curiosity

The fuel that lights the fire of connectivity is pure curiosity.

One of the observations I have made about my clients that are able to learn to raise their performance is their ability to become super curious about other people.

The driver of this has multiple dimensions.

Firstly, when they learn to learn, they recognise that becoming curious about what others are doing yields great learning results. It's much easier to learn from the real-time experiences of others than to make your own mistakes or study information from other sources which, in this fast-moving world, can so often turn out to be dated already. People who originally stated that they hated going to networking events or social functions suddenly become adept conversationalists as they feed off the rich steam of ideas that others have to offer. They are surprised by what others will willingly share if you just ask in the right way and say thank you afterwards. Whilst it still takes mental effort to attend these events, particularly for less outgoing types, it is very rare that you go to an event and don't learn something useful – if you apply a sense of curiosity.

If you go and talk about yourself all night, or only talk to people you already know well or hide in the kitchen, then you will learn what you deserve to learn – not much!

As important as learning is, curiosity also yields up something even more valuable. This is the discovery of people who think like you. People who share your values. People who get excited about achieving similar things that you want to achieve. People who could become your colleagues, employees, followers, customers, mentors, partners. People who can become part of your tribe.

You may be thinking that the idea of 'knowing the right people' is nothing new. However, there is a big difference between making an acquaintance and creating a relationship. You can meet hundreds of people superficially and exchange polite conversation. You can get to know what they do and where they live, etc. But how many of these people do you get to know well enough to understand how they think and what their value set is. This is where true curiosity comes in. If you are genuinely curious about others, then you develop the skill of asking great questions that dig deep into someone's life quite quickly. Every time you find common emotional ground, you can make a connection that is meaningful for both parties.

Questions such as the following, tend to receive superficial answers because people are practised at answering these questions:

What do you do?

How long have you been doing that for?

Where do you live?

Do you have kids?

They are likely to have answered them hundreds of times before.

So, more curiosity-based questions are ones like:

Why did you choose to do that?

Is that what you always wanted to do?

Is it working out for you as you hoped?

How do you see yourself in 5 years from now?

What's the grand plan?

What is it about what you do that really excites you?

These questions make people think and, as a result, a much more interesting conversation happens. Often, people have not been asked these types of questions before and often the resultant thoughts ignite emotions. Emotion is great for starting a relationship. Without spurring emotion, you can't really start to understand someone well or build any emotional bonds.

Your black book

The result of high curiosity is that you start to build up a whole set of people that either directly or indirectly can help you in some way.

I recommend you store these valuable assets in a version of your personal 'black book'. This is your database of contacts that you want to nurture. Stay in contact with them and find ways to interact with them as much as possible. Invite them to events, send them interesting bits of information that might help them, join their group of contacts in LinkedIn or Facebook, send them referrals to people they could do business with.

Remember a good relationship has to be reciprocal. The more you give, the more you get back in return.

Compiling your black book is not just about the people you have already met, but also have a section for all the people you want to meet. Be pro-active in working out who you would like to connect with in the area in which you want to progress.

This requires some research first.

For instance, if you want to become a great tennis player in the area in which you live, then researching all the best local tennis coaches would be a good start.

If you want to swim The Channel or climb Everest then researching who has recently done this in your sphere of contacts and reaching out to them would be very valuable.

Never assume that people will not want to talk to you. You don't get anything if you don't ask and you will be surprised that most of the time people will respond to the power of curiosity.

Also, never assume that people don't want to talk to you if they don't respond first time, or even the second or third. Alongside **curiosity** is her twin brother **persistence**. Often people are just busy or you did not get them at a convenient time. During my time working in a sales role, I learned that sometimes it takes many attempts to connect with someone. It just takes the right time and the right occasion. This takes some mental resilience because you are probably telling yourself the story that you are not worthy of that person taking their valuable time to interact with you. The feeling of rejection can be debilitating; it eats away at your self-confidence. I urge you to totally ignore this version of the story. Find a better story.

The best I heard is from the book by Frank Bettger – *How I Raised Myself from Failure to Success in Selling.*

He tells his own story of failing in the role as an insurance sales man. He returned to it a while later and learned to be an outstanding success. One of his learnings was to keep accurate records of every sales call he made. His mindset changed once he realised it was a numbers game. For every 2.5 calls he made he got an interview, and for every 12 interviews he got a sale. He concluded that he made $2.40 for every call he made in those early days. As he perfected his technique, that rose to $20 per call. Once he had it in his head that every call made him money regardless of whether anyone responded or not, his success grew and grew as did his motivation to make more calls.

The connectivity mindset is exactly the same. The more people you talk to, the more you connect with. A new conversation is never a waste of time, it's just another step towards finding the right people to connect with. Don't worry if you have to try on multiple occasions. The maths will look after you.

Black book exercise:

Write a list of people who you would like to get to know.

The people I would like to know well.	Why do I want to know them?

Influence and attraction

Interacting well with the right people and building relationships with them is a great skill in its own right. The next tier of skill is the ability to influence them in a way that attracts them to support your cause.

We are all influenced by the people around us in some way but what is it that attracts us to certain people in a way that motivates us to help them or become part of the sphere of activity that they are involved in?

The essence of influence is very similar to the essence of leadership. Great leaders are people that others are prepared to follow.

We want to attract people to follow us, to help us and believe in us. This gives us the strength and support to achieve those things that would be totally out of reach if we were acting alone.

So, the most straightforward guide to personal influence and attraction is to adopt the well-known model that great leaders have used over the years. This is to develop a personal **Vision**, a **Mission** and a set of personal **Values**.

Your personal vision is an aspirational picture of what you want to achieve. A picture that excites you, but more importantly excites others to such a degree that they want to participate and share in this vision. Something big enough that you will be remembered for. Your legacy to your family and the world.

The examples of personal visions are endless, but here are a few:

- *To eradicate homelessness in the town in which I live and love.*
- *To build a renowned and respected family wine business that will last for generations to come.*
- *To become the first person from my town to compete in the Olympic Games.*
- *To give all children in my hometown in Africa access to free education in a safe environment.*
- *To become the most famous and most loved cake shop in South West England.*

All of these create a vivid picture of a future that benefits others; a goal that without you would probably never happen, but one that you cannot achieve alone.

When you are truly excited by your personal vision and talk about it to others with great enthusiasm then those who relate to it will start to engage with you and move to the next stage of engagement: the mission. Enthusiasm is a vital ingredient here. Enthusiasm in itself acts as a magnet that can draw people towards the warmth of its glow.

It also acts as a filter. Those people who don't relate to it at all will not react and so you can move on quickly and apply your curiosity to others.

The mission is the part that gives the vision believability. The mission paints a picture of exactly how you are going to achieve your mission. The techniques, the resources, the people that will be deployed to achieve the over-arching goal.

Let's take the first example:

To eradicate homelessness in the town in which I live and love.

The mission behind this might be:

We create and coordinate a body of local business owners who care as much as we do. We know that unemployment is the biggest cause of homelessness, so we run dynamic programmes to help the vulnerable to become people who obtain and sustain a proper job. We have a number of hostels to keep people off the streets, but people who stay in our hostels are obliged to undertake learning activities within the programme during the day. We believe that every single person in our town, with the benefit of this support can sustain themselves and, moreover, contribute to our community.

When you hear this, then you know that there is substance behind the vision. This substance makes it tangible and believable. Underneath, people want to be involved with activities that are going to be successful and will provide a sense of achievement and fulfillment to those who choose to lend their energy and commitment to the cause. Without a strong mission then a vision is just a crazy fantastical personal dream that other people are unlikely to buy into.

The most influential pieces of the jigsaw are your values and beliefs. If you think of creating connectivity through creating your own personal brand, then your values and beliefs are, in effect, your brand attributes.

Interestingly, in today's world of social media, there is a whole new profession as an 'influencer'. These influencers have a huge following as people buy into their authority in certain areas (fashion, food, music, etc) but, more importantly, they also buy into their values and beliefs. They relate to their 'way of thinking' and hence are prepared to follow them.

When you influence the way people think, then this is the most powerful form of influence. We use the term 'thought leaders' in society not by accident. It's these types of leaders that gain the biggest influence on what happens in our world. The politicians, religious leaders, the technology pioneers, the humanists, the scientists etc – the people that think ahead and encourage others to think with them.

Coming back to our personal values and beliefs, then the same applies to your ability to influence. If you have a value and belief set that people want to be part of, and is more compelling than their own, then you have moved someone to a better place. This movement that you have created is the essence of influence.

As a coach, this represents a big part of my role. I don't attempt to guide people on what to DO, but to teach them to think in a better way. If your thinking is right, then the doing is easy.

One of my clients is developing a vegan food business. She has a very strong belief set around healthy eating, living well and creating balance in life. She attracts very talented people to her team who share her views, her values and her beliefs. She is going to build a quality and successful business because she can attract passionate and driven people that connect with both her and her vision at an emotional level – a level that is far more powerful than any rational reasons to work with her company. This also applies to her customers who are, in effect, her followers. They love the idea of the type of lifestyle she vividly paints in her communication and, as a result, they purchase her products because her core idea aligns with their value and belief set.

So, what are your strongly-held personal values and beliefs that if you communicate them well would attract talented, passionate people to help you?

Just to give you a couple of examples, let me share with you a couple of mine.

- I believe strongly that everyone can shape their own future and be what they want to be. I express it using a couple of phrases: *Where there's a will there's a way*, or, *You can be what you will to be.* People around me know that I always encourage this thinking and that I don't accept excuses or limiting beliefs around this area.

- I believe strongly in positive thinking. I don't worry about things that I can't control or things that have already happened. I believe that anyone can choose their response to any difficult situation, hence I don't accept negativity. I express this with the expression, *Live above the line.* People around me understand exactly what I mean when I use this term.

Values and beliefs exercise

I believe that …
The phrase I use to express this is …

I believe that …
The phrase I use to express this is …

I believe that …
The phrase I use to express this is …

I believe that …
The phrase I use to express this is …

I believe that …
The phrase I use to express this is …

I believe that …
The phrase I use to express this is …

Communication

We connect with people through our powers of communication.

Others judge us remarkably quickly by the way we present ourselves, both in our body language and what we say.

Our communication style is wholly driven by our thoughts at the time in which we engage with others. If you are greeting an old friend or lover then your head and heart is full of joy and this immediately comes across in the way we physically communicate. If you are talking to someone you don't like or respect and you are thinking that you would rather to be somewhere else, then this thought 'leaks' very quickly into your communication. The other person will almost certainly detect these 'leaks' unless you are a very good actor.

We have covered in some depth our ability to manage our thoughts in any type of situation. It follows then that we are able to manage our communication style for every situation.

As an exercise, ask someone to be your partner and greet them in four different ways.

- In a manner in which you are just casually saying hello to a work colleague in the morning, but you have a few things on your mind.
- In a manner in which you are really pleased to see them. Like a long-lost friend.
- In a manner in which you feel you are more important than they are.
- In a manner in which you feel really depressed today.

What you realise very quickly is that you can have a massive impact on others by choosing the state on mind in which you approach them.

Whether it's a one-to-one encounter, a phone call, if you are walking into a room or if you are presenting on stage, the way you choose to 'set' yourself will shape the way you are able to connect with others.

Being mindful of the impact of the first approach and proactively taking a pause before engaging to *set yourself* properly for the encounter is a habit that will greatly improve your connectivity.

Tips for setting yourself:

The first thing that others are sensitive to is how **present** you are with them. If you are giving signals that you really want to be there with them, then you can create connectivity. If others perceive that you are indifferent about being in the encounter, then connectivity lines are not created or are quickly broken.

Bad habits such as looking at your smartphone whilst in a meeting or conversation are instant connectivity killers. This is broadcasting the fact that you are more interested in other communication rather than communicating with them.

Great communication requires both parties to be fully present with each other and give each other certain reassurance signals to convince them that is the case. The nods, the notes taken, the questions, the admiration, the expressions of interest, etc.

The biggest factor here is maintaining eye contact. This requires mental focus and concentration, but is the one sure-fire way to signal to others that you are fully present with them. This applies to both groups and individuals. The only difference being that you have to deliberately pick out people to form eye contact with in a group and rotate this focus around the room to communicate to the wider group that you are focused wholly on them.

When setting yourself for achieving presence then you will need to mentally and emotionally commit to the encounter, discarding any competing activities that could distract you and destroy the line of connectivity you are trying to build.

You are achieving presence when you are truly connecting with the thoughts and emotions of others. When you are in this zone, you are optimising your level of connectivity.

Enthusiasm is the other component of creating a connection. It's the electricity in the cables that create the connections.

We all relate to enthusiasm in life. We admire it in others and crave it for ourselves. It is a happy emotion that acts as a magnet to draw others towards us.

Just like being present, this requires a conscious decision to be enthusiastic in your encounters as often, natural enthusiasm just does not come along at the same time as when we need to connect with someone. Acting enthusiastic when building your communication skills is fine. We all have acting skills that we can turn on and off. Whilst this might sound a bit 'false', it is a means to an end. What you are actually doing is building an enthusiasm habit by practising the 'act' over thousands of occasions. After a while, we become habitually enthusiastic in our communications. Imagine the amount of connections you will make over a life-time if you approach all your communications with enthusiasm rather than just those where you happen to be feeling enthusiastic at the time? The difference is immense.

The third component is to become mindful of what your *body language* is communicating to others. To connect with another person, the body language of both people needs to be both open and matched. Just like adapting to the DISC profile of the other person, you also need to adapt to their mode of body language.

If you watch two people meeting each other, you will often see them 'matching and mirroring' each other's body positions and facial expressions. If one person leans on the table the other will match; if one takes a drink the other will follow; if one touches her face the other will match; if one crosses their legs the other will follow. Next time you are in a café or restaurant have fun to observing others. If you watch carefully, you will see people who don't know each other well and are trying to connect. You will see their match and mirror behaviours. When you meet someone next for a coffee who you don't know so well, try making distinct movements and see if they match and mirror you.

This is natural behaviour between two human beings who want to connect with each other. It's a communication ritual which can either work and a connection occurs, or fail and no relationship takes root.

When you are mindful of this you can adopt 'open' body language from the very beginning. Open your posture, don't cross your arms or hunch your shoulders. This is guarded body language that filters and blocks connectivity. Smile and open your arms and chest to welcome open communication. The other person will almost certainly match and connectivity can flow.

With people you already know well, and in relaxed situations, you don't feel the need to match and mirror. They are already connected to you. They do, however, tend to revert to this behaviour in more difficult encounters, when they don't feel as confident with you and need to re-establish a good connection to communicate effectively. If you know this, then you can detect if people feel slightly uncomfortable with you. You can see the signs and take corrective body positions to put them at ease.

Lastly, the content of how you introduce yourself is important. You often only get a short chance to make an impression that attracts the other person to want to engage with you. The key here is to be *concise and impactful* with your communication.

Often, you don't get many opportunities to make an impression, and these opportunities can be very short. If you have practised a number of well thought out ways of presenting yourself and your ideas, then you can take full advantage of every opportunity you get. If you don't prepare and just use whatever comes to you at the time the chance is that you will ramble, or use lazy words and phrases that do not engage or explain your key messages.

Great politicians are good examples of this. Love him or hate him, Donald Trump is a master of the well-crafted, impactful phrase. Closer to home, Boris Johnson is an amazing orator. His use of words to make impact is an art he works very hard on. He understands how this amplifies his message, amplifies his impact and hence his ability to influence others.

I love quotations from great people, particularly people such as Winston Churchill, Nelson Mandela and Mother Teresa. If you think about it, these were just their well-designed pieces of concise and impactful communication, which were so powerful that they still have impact today.

So, to build your ability to influence and attract, start to build your portfolio of concise and impactful ways of communicating your message.

These could be ideas backed by short stories, or anecdotes. Or they could be ideas backed by famous quotations. Vivid examples that illustrate your message. Or a colourful way of painting a picture in people's minds of the aspirational dream that you have.

This portfolio will give you the confidence that, whatever communication opportunities that come your way, you have the tools prepared and ready in your toolbox to be able to deliver and attract great connections.

One of the key opportunities is how you introduce yourself. If it takes you ten sentences to describe yourself, then you have almost certainly lost the opportunity to connect. These introductions define your identity and explore whether there is any common ground.

A good way to do this is to write a number of versions of your personal story in long hand, then try and summarise them in just a single sentence. Have a go. It is remarkably difficult and can take many attempts to find sentences that are concise and have impact.

Here are a few examples:

I tell stories to children around the world. (An internationally-renowned writer and television producer).

I help people lead healthy and vibrant lives. (A personal trainer and nutritional specialist).

I deliver sustainable, clean energy for people across the globe. (The owner of a solar power and battery company that builds clean energy plants for electric vehicle charging and telecom towers).

These concise phrases have impact and invite the other person to respond with:

That's interesting, how do you do that?

or

Tell me more.

They engage the listener and invite them in if they want to explore, rather than imposing a long story on them.

Great 'connectors' have a number of these concise introduction phrases that they use in different situations with different types of people. They draw people in, then invite them to peel back the layers of their story at a pace that they control.

When creating these, remember that they have to be fully authentic to you. Anything that is 'put on just for show' will alienate rather than attract. It's about creating words that attract people in to find out more about the real you and everything you have to offer in terms of investing in a relationship.

So, what are your concise and impactful introduction sentences?

I ...

I...

I...

I...

Communicating to groups

When you communicate to groups of people, you can greatly amplify your impact and influence.

The truth is that most people are petrified of public-speaking and admire others that are prepared to do it, provided, of course, that they do it well.

It is one of those skills that it pays to master if you want to leverage your capacity to connect with others.

Let's take the example of you attending an event with 30 people in the room. There may be only one that could be a fantastic connection for you. To find this person, you will have to find a way to have a meaningful conversation with all 30. This is practically and socially very difficult without appearing pushy and self-important and hence the opportunity is often missed. However, if you have the opportunity to address the whole group with a concise and engaging address, then this person will find you afterwards. Not only that, but you have established your identity and credibility so this person is motivated to engage with you in a positive fashion.

You might be thinking to yourself that you are not good at public speaking, or that the very thought of it fills you with dread.

I have met many people who start with this mindset but quickly learn how to become really strong public speakers. Like any skill, it just takes knowledge and practice.

Let's start with the structure of what you are going to say. If this is well-constructed, then you have confidence about your content and you can be sure the audience has information in a form they can understand and digest.

I was lucky enough to work with a really talented communication specialist. She had studied the art of making great presentations and created a simple structure that works effectively to help anyone to improve their public speaking.

The first stage is grabbing the attention of the audience and giving them a reason to listen. Being dramatic in some sense is required at this stage. You can lose an audience very quickly if your introduction is not impactful.

Speakers use a variety of techniques to do this:

- A question, followed by a long pause.
- A dramatic image followed by a question.
- A controversial statement.
- A compliment to the audience.
- A joke with an underlying message.

Whatever you choose, it must grab the attention of your audience, cause them to sit up and say to themselves 'I'd better listen to this, it sounds interesting.' The temptation is to start cautiously to ease yourself into it, however this is totally counter-productive as you quickly start to sense your audience is not engaged, which then has the effect of eroding your confidence and the going becomes even tougher.

Once you have engaged your audience, then divide your content into just three themes. People cannot absorb or remember large quantities of information. Three themes hit the sweet spot between having enough content to fulfill the audience and not too much to overwhelm them. It's best to tell them upfront that you are going to cover only three themes, so they know what's coming and know they only have to listen out for these. If they don't know what's coming, then they can't prepare and tend not to absorb information effectively as it appears as random information in a random order.

If, after covering your three themes, you want to take questions from the audience then make sure you do this before you present your conclusion.

An impactful conclusion is critical for securing the actions and reactions you want to leave your listeners with. It must be the last thing that the audience hears from you.

If you attempt to conclude prior to taking questions, then the audience is left hearing a discussion between you and a member of the audience, rather that a well-planned and executed final conclusion.

So, start strong, cover three themes, take questions and finish strong. Simple!

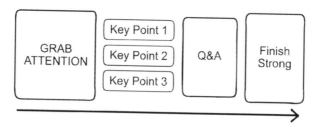

This covers the basic structure of the address, but what about the nature of the content? Before starting to draft your address, decide exactly how you want your audience to feel at the end of the address.

Do you want them to feel: reassured, excited, terrified, included, or committed to act? Remember you are trying to influence your audience, so it's important to plan how your language is going to do this.

A useful model for this was provided by none other than the ancient Greek philosopher and scientist Aristotle. His model of persuasion is as relevant today as it was back then.

He maintained there are three lines of persuasion.

Firstly, Ethos. This is about the characteristics of the speaker – whether you have enough credibility to influence and persuade and whether you have a style that can engage the audience.

In most cases you will need to share a degree of your story to build this credibility with the audience. Demonstrate that you have earned the right to be talking to them on the subject. If you fail to do this, then you will not have enough gravitas to be able to generate the action or reaction you are seeking.

Composing your story could be a whole chapter in its own right, but for the purpose of this book it's enough to say that it's an essential part of the script that needs to be woven into the text.

Typically, speakers weave in their success stories, and the success stories of the clients and teams they have worked with. You can also include stories of failure, to demonstrate that you have life experience and have benefited from learning from your mistakes. The art here is not to brag, but to use each story to add a layer of interest and learning for your audience whilst sub-consciously building your own credibility in their minds.

Your mode of delivery also plays a large part in Ethos. When you deliver with confidence, with impact, and also provide the audience both education and entertainment, then your credibility rises.

Then comes Logos, which is the strength of your message. The logical, fact-based reasons that appeal to your left brain.

This is the depth of your content. It's here that facts, figures, statistics, and examples are used to build the logical spine of your argument. As we have discussed earlier, this element has a different weighting with different parts of the audience. For the more task-orientated individuals, Logos is the core of what will persuade them of your arguments.

Finally, comes Pathos which is the emotional part of persuasion. This is the part where you are using the emotions of your audience to influence them. Depending on how you want to leave them feeling, you can leverage a whole scope of different emotions such as love, fear, greed, frustration, unity, anger, respect, etc. This requires not only the use of emotional language, but often a bit of acting to stimulate the emotions of your audience.

If you listen to accomplished connectors, you will start to recognise Ethos, Logos and Pathos in the way they communicate. Now that you are aware of the method, you can make notes on what elements resonate with you and start to build and practise your own communication tool box.

Aristotle's Model of Persuasion

LOGOS
The Content
(logic & facts)

ETHOS
The Speaker
(credibility &
charisma)

PATHOS
The Emotion
(How you want the
audience to feel)

Being an effective communicator and influencer also requires control of your voice. Think of the amount of times your connection opportunity comes over the phone and you don't have the benefit of body language. All the work has to be done with your voice.

When approaching these opportunities, it's important to manage your mood before you engage. Your mood will reflect directly in your voice and the response you get from the other person.

A positive and enthusiastic mood will achieve a very different result from a cautious and thoughtful mood. Be mindful of the outcome you want and pro-actively set your mood to achieve this result.

This checklist is a useful prompt for managing your voice.

V – olume.

A – rticulation

P – itch

E – mphasis

R – ate

For VOLUME don't be afraid to turn it up. It may sound to you that you are almost shouting. However, volume brings more energy and ensures that everyone in the room can actually hear what you are saying. If you are too quiet, people are often too polite to admit they cannot hear properly and hence your opportunity is lost for these individuals.

For ARTICULATION make sure that you finish your words correctly. The biggest error is being lazy when articulating every word, which leaves your audience having to fill the gaps in what they are hearing. When this happens, they often take a different meaning to what you intended. Listen to the newsreaders on TV and radio and note how they take care to do this.

For PITCH it's important to vary it. If you talk with the same pitch, then people switch off. Babies use up to 28 different notes to communicate with, whereas adults tend to use only 3 in their normal communication. If you practice varying the pitch of your voice then your range will improve and you will be a more engaging communicator.

For EMPHASIS be mindful of where the emphasis is in a sentence. Changing the word on which the emphasis is placed changes the meaning of a sentence.

For example, the sentence: 'We had three opportunities to tell him he was wrong.'

If you put emphasis on *three,* then the sentence is all about the opportunities missed.

If you put the emphasis on *wrong,* then the sentence is about him being wrong.

It's often required to exaggerate emphasis to create both clarity and effect. Using pauses also underlines where you want the emphasis to lie.

For RATE the temptation is **always** to speak too fast, particularly when you are slightly nervous. You will always hear yourself at a faster rate than your audience, because your thinking is running ahead of what you are saying. If you slow down your rate you gain more control of your delivery, and with this control comes better impact.

It's also worth remembering that when addressing a group, or a large audience, it will contain many different types of people who relate to different things. Many will be different to you, so building in all these elements can often feel un-natural to you. The thing to always remind yourself of is that it's not about you sounding good to yourself, it's about getting the desired response from the audience you are addressing.

Your communication can ONLY be judged on the response you get from your audience. If you get the response you wanted, then you have communicated well. If you don't, then you have not.

Plan to connect

Finally, a word on planning your connectivity activities.

You will do only what you schedule in your diary. If it's important to you to connect with others and build up your black book, then the activities that will lead to this outcome need to be planned. Don't leave it to chance.

Ask yourself:

What structured time will I set aside for networking?

What structured time will I set aside for connecting with others on LinkedIn and Facebook?

Which industry events will I attend?

What group presentations will I do, to what audience?

What structured time will I spend crafting my introductions, my vision, mission and values?

The art of connectivity requires a personal investment in thought, structure and, above all, practice. In my experience, the pay-back on this investment is always a handsome one.

Exercise:

Rate yourself on the Connectivity Checklist (below) and evaluate where you are today and what you need to work on.

Connectivity Checklist

Areas	Score (1-5) (1 = No, 5= Absolutely Yes)
Understanding People Do I understand my own behavioural profile? Can I read others quickly and accurately? Do I know what type of people complement me? Do I mindfully adapt my behaviour to connect with others? *Curiosity* Do I practice curiosity with everyone I meet? Do I have an active Black Book? *Influence and Attraction* Do I have a compelling personal vision? Do I have a believable personal mission? Do I have strong values and beliefs that attract others? *Communication* Do I mindfully 'set' myself before communicating? Do I have a tool kit of rehearsed set pieces? Do I seek opportunities to address audiences? Do I take time to structure my speeches well? Do I deliver my speeches with impact?	
Total	

PART THREE

PERSONAL PRODUCTIVITY

Personal Productivity

Have you ever wondered why some people seem to keep lots of activities on the go at one time, and are successful at all of them! Meanwhile, you have a never-ending to-do list, never having the time to finish things properly, never having time to do some of the things you really want to do and frequently getting stressed about feeling overworked.

The answer is quite simple, in that they have built a personal productivity system that allows them to leverage their time in such a way that they can achieve much more in a day than you are doing. Richard Branson has 12 hours in every day – exactly the same amount of time as you and I have – but he runs a multitude of businesses, charities, homes and other activities in his 12 hours. He just has a better method than you do.

Developing your own personal productivity system is going to be an essential part of you improving your performance. Just imagine the impact of achieving 50% more out of every day than you do today.

The core principle of achieving this is the principle of Proactivity.

The principle of proactivity

The core idea behind achieving high levels of productivity is one of proactively deciding what you are going to spend your time on.

If you often feel like life is happening to you, rather than you are living your life in the way you want to live it, then you are allowing yourself to live in a reactive mode. Time is not your own, your time belongs to many other people around you. You have effectively ceded control to others.

For some reason, we allow ourselves some great excuses with regard to this:
'I am really not great at time management'

or

'Time just seems to run away with me'.

However, if you think about it, the way you use your time is about making a series of decisions. The quality of these decisions governs what you achieve in the day. So time management is actually decision management. So, if I ask you how good you are at making decisions, would you allow yourself the same latitude in terms of excuses?

Achieving high levels of productivity depends on developing the habit of **you** proactively deciding **what** you are going to do and **when** you are going to do it.

Of course, there are occasions when things don't go to plan and you have to react. Have you ever noticed, however, how proactive, organised people have significantly less disasters than reactive, disorganised people?

The first part of developing the habit is identifying what are your High Value Activities (HVA's). These are the activities that are going to add the most value to your life.

These are the things that are both your critical anchors that give you balance and those things that are important to achieve the key progression goals you have set yourself.

For example, your balance HVA's might include:

- Going to the gym 3 times per week.
- Doing yoga twice per week.
- Putting the children to bed every evening.
- Eating out with your partner twice per week.
- Reading for an hour every day.
- Playing hockey twice per week.
- Seeing your parents twice per month.
- Cooking a great meal for the family on a Sunday.

These activities are what you personally need to stay balanced and to be able to perform at a high level in the vocational aspects of your life.

Once our non-negotiable balance HVA's are defined, we move onto our work or vocational HVA's.

These can be more difficult to figure out.

Start by asking yourself a few questions:
What activities do I love doing that really create value using the expertise I have?
What activities do I love doing, but could really be done by anyone else?
What activities do I not like doing, but require a high level of expertise and are important to what I do?
What activities do I not like doing and could be done by anyone.

Then list them in this matrix.

Skill / Fun Matrix

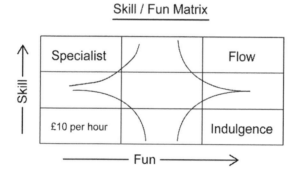

The top right-hand corner is where you are in 'flow' and you should aim to spend as much time as you can in this zone. You are enjoying work and making big strides along your chosen path.

The bottom right is 'indulgent'. You love these activities, you are good at them, but others can do these things just as well. So, move out of this zone into the flow zone. It's just as much fun, but moves you much further forward.

The top left is your 'specialist' box. These activities should not be done by you but by specialists that will do it much better than you can. If you try and play in this box, you are accepting a mediocre performance in an important area. Much better to pay better qualified people to do a first-class job and spend your time in the flow box.

The bottom left box is your '£10 per hour box'. These are low-skilled jobs that you don't like and you can pay others to do at a low cost. If you are doing these tasks, then you are effectively valuing your time at '£10 per hour' rather than the rate you can earn in the flow box.

Once you have put all your activities in these boxes, start work from the bottom LH corner and move towards the top RH corner. Progressively re-allocate these activities to others until you arrive at your optimum place – in the 'flow' zone.

Your current skill / fun situation

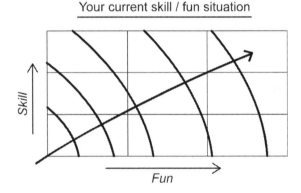

Exercise:

I am going to reduce my £10 per hour work by taking the following actions:

  1.
  2.
  3.
  4.

I am going to stop doing the skilled work that I don't enjoy by taking the following actions:

1.
2.
3.
4.

I am going to delegate the following things that I enjoy but know can be done by others:

1.
2.
3.
4.

If you are not exactly sure of what constitute HVA's, consider the Steven Covey's urgent/important matrix from his legendary book, *The Seven Habits of Highly-Effective People*. He plots activities across the axis of URGENT and IMPORTANT.

Urgent ↑	Delusion	Demand
	Distraction	The Zone

Important →

Similar to the skill/fun matrix, the bottom LH quadrant is just **distraction** (not urgent and not important). All those hours responding to emails, browsing the web, social media, taking random calls, etc. These are time sinks that destroy your personal productivity.

The top LH quadrant is just **delusion** (urgent but not important). This is time spent dealing with things that are urgent to people around you but don't move you forward. This is caused mainly by 'superhumanitis' – the emotion that makes you feel good because you love to feel needed. You feel like you are the go-to person who heroically solves problems, and deals with crisis for the people around you. The cure for 'superhumanitis' is learning to coach the people around you to plan better and solve their own problems. If you do this, people soon learn that if they come to you, they will receive help and challenge on how to solve their own problems rather than someone who will take the problem away from them. After a while, most of these requests disappear as people get better at removing the cause of issues or thinking for themselves and taking personal accountability for solving their own issues. Your position is actually enhanced because you elevate yourself into the 'wise coach' position and also grow the capability of the people around you. It's a win-win scenario.

A good technique for doing this is to use the GROW model.

G is for goal. Ask the other person to clarify the goal. The desired outcome.
R is for reality. Ask the other person to define the facts pertinent to the situation.
O is for options. Ask the other person for multiple suggestions on how the problem could be solved.
W is for way forward. Ask the other person to decide which of their options they believe is best. Then give them permission and encouragement to go and take this action themselves.

You will notice that this requires you just to ask a series of questions in the correct order that guides the other person to resolving their own problem.

The top RH quadrant is *demand* (urgent and important). This is where you are delivering the core thing that you do. If you are an athlete you are training or competing; if you are doctor you are directly helping patients; if you are an actor you are rehearsing or performing, etc. These core activities are clearly essential and should occupy at least 50% of your time, however if they are absorbing the majority of your time you are probably not moving forward.

The quadrant that moves you forward is the *zone* quadrant (not urgent but important). These activities are developing and improving you and what you do.

They are activities such as:

- Learning
- Reflection
- Planning
- Recruiting
- Developing people around you
- Connecting with people who can help you
- Systemising demand activities, so others can take them on
- Seeking and absorbing feedback from people around you

By definition, these activities are not urgent. If you don't do them there are no immediate consequences. However, it's **only** these activities that will drive your performance and progression. The more time you are able to spend in the *zone,* the faster you will progress.

So, the trick is to try and eliminate, as much as possible, the time spent in the *distraction* and *delusion* quadrants, keep the time in the *demand* quadrant to a manageable level and proactively invest the rest of your time in the *zone.*

When considering your *zone* activities ask yourself the question.

What are the one or two things that, if I did them consistently well, would move me forward at the fastest rate?

These will be your ultra HVA's that deserve your maximum focus and attention.

Exercises:

It's really useful to do a time study on a few actual weeks. Just record what you are actually spending your time on. Then transfer the information into the following table. You will be amazed at how much time you can divert into activities that move you forward faster.

My distractions. (eg email, social media, answering calls)	Actions to stop wasting time on these	Time per week I could save

People who often dump urgent issues on me	Actions to stop this happening	Time per week I could save

My core 'demand' activities	How much time do I spend on each per week?	How much time should I spend on each per week?

My key 'zone' activities	How much time do I spend on each per week?	How much time should I spend on each per week?

A tool to help you manage your HVA's

At this point you should have established your HVA's.

These will be your *balance* HVA's plus your *zone* HVA's and finally your *demand* HVA's.

If you proactively prioritise your time on these activities every week over all other demands on your time, then your personal productivity will rise significantly.

The tool we use to do this is called our 'perfect week' diary.

It's called this because it's a template for what we want every week to look like.

Once we have designed our PW diary, then the task is simply to try and plan every actual week to be as close as possible to this template.

Below is an example of a PW diary for a client of mine. She owns a busy design business with a team of 6 people.

	Mon	Tue	Wed	Thur	Fri
7-8am	Exercise Class	**Networking**	Exercise Class		Exercise Class
8-9am	*Breakfast*	**Networking**	*Breakfast*	*Breakfast*	*Breakfast*
9-10am	**1-1 Meetings**	Team Meeting	Client Meetings	**Research**	Design
10-11am	**1-1 Meetings**	Team Meeting	Client Meetings	**Research**	Design
11-12pm	**1-1 Meetings**		Client Meetings	**Research**	Design
12-1pm	**1-1 Meetings**	Coaching	Client Meetings	**Research**	Design
1-1.30pm	*Lunch*	*Lunch*	*Lunch*	*Lunch*	*Lunch*
1.30-2.pm	*Email/VM's*	*Email/VM's*	*Email/VM's*	*Email/VM's*	*Email/VM's*
2-3pm	Project Reviews	Design	Prospect Meetings	Site Visits	Design
3-4pm	Project Reviews	Design	Prospect Meetings	Site Visits	Design
4-5pm	Project Reviews	Design	Prospect Meetings	Site Visits	Design
5-5.30pm	*Email/VM's*	*Email/VM's*	*Email/VM's*	*Email/VM's*	*Email/VM's*
5.30-6pm	**Daily Planning**	**Daily Planning**	**Daily Planning**	**Daily Planning**	**Daily Planning**
6-7pm					
7-8pm	Yoga		Yoga		Dinner Out
8-9pm	Yoga		Yoga		Dinner Out
9-10pm					Dinner Out

Activity Breakdown

Balance HVA's	Hrs	Demand HVA's	Hrs	Zone HVA's	Hrs
Exercise	3	Project Reviews	3	1-1 Meetings	4
Yoga	4	Design	9	Team Meeting	2
Dinner Out	3	Client Meetings	3	Coaching	1
		Site Visits	3	Research	4
		Prospect meetings	3	Planning	2.5
				Networking	2
Total	10		21		15.5

You can see that she leaves very little room for 'distraction'. Emails and VM's are kept to 2 x half-hour slots every day.

'Delusion' is also kept to a minimum as there is quality time allocated to both 1-1 and team meetings. The team know they have this dedicated time with her, so they don't need her to solve their problems for the rest of the week.

This leaves a high proportion of time available for her Demand and Zone activities.

She also values her balance activities and books them in advance as outside classes so she is not tempted to skip them. She knows that these activities keep her in good shape, both mentally and physically.

Of course, every real week is a little different. However, her PA knows her PW (it is a coloured chart on her wall) and books out her week so it is as close as possible to this ideal, hence maximising her personal productivity.

Here is another example of an Athlete. She is a GB rower with very different HVA's.

	Mon	Tue	Wed	Thur	Fri
7-8am	Stretching	Stretching	Stretching	Stretching	Stretching
8-9am	*Rowing*	*Rowing*	*Rowing*	*Rowing*	*Rowing*
9-10am	*Rowing*	*Rowing*	*Rowing*	*Rowing*	*Rowing*
10-11am	*Breakfast*	*Breakfast*	*Breakfast*	*Breakfast*	*Breakfast*
11-12pm	*Rowing*	*Rowing*	*Rowing*	*Rowing*	*Rowing*
12-1pm	*Rowing*	*Rowing*	*Rowing*	*Rowing*	*Rowing*
1-1.30pm	*Lunch*	*Lunch*	*Lunch*	*Lunch*	*Lunch*
1.30-2.pm	Physiotherapy	Reviewing	Reviewing	Physiotherapy	Reviewing
2-3pm	*Weight Lifting*	*Weight Lifting*	Work (Office)	*Weight Lifting*	*Weight Lifting*
3-4pm	*Weight Lifting*	*Weight Lifting*	Work (Office)	*Weight Lifting*	*Weight Lifting*
4-5pm			Work (Office)		
5-5.30pm	Work (Home)	Work (Home)		Work (Home)	Work (Home)
5.30-6pm	Work (Home)	Work (Home)		Work (Home)	Work (Home)
6-7pm	Relaxing	Relaxing	Relaxing	Relaxing	Relaxing
7-8pm	*Dinner*	*Dinner*	*Dinner*	*Dinner*	*Dinner*
8-9pm	Daily Planning	Daily Planning	Daily Planning	Daily Planning	Relaxing
9-10pm	Relaxing	Relaxing	Relaxing	Relaxing	Relaxing

Balance HVA's	Hrs	Demand HVA's	Hrs	Zone HVA's	Hrs
Relaxing	11	Rowing	20	Physiotherapy	1
Work (Home)	4	Weight Lifting	8	Stretching	5
Work (Office)	3			Reviewing	1.5
				Planning	4
Total	18		28		11.5

Her Perfect Week diary is more defined as she is in an elite training regime aiming to compete in the Tokyo Olympics. Note the rest and reflection time in her PW, this recovery activity is really important for everyone regardless of your vocation.

Exercise:

Design Your Own PW Diary.

	Mon	Tue	Wed	Thur	Fri
7-8am					
8-9am					
9-10am					
10-11am					
11-12pm					
12-1pm					
1-1.30pm					
1.30-2.pm					
2-3pm					
3-4pm					
4-5pm					
5-5.30pm					
5.30-6pm					
6-7pm					
7-8pm					
8-9pm					
9-10pm					

Activity Breakdown

Balance HVA's	Hrs	Demand HVA's	Hrs	Zone HVA's	Hrs
Total					

Effective Goal Setting

The second area where the power of proactivity shines is effective goal setting.

Most of us are good at achieving things when what we want or need to achieve is really clearly defined and we are excited about the benefits of achieving it.

We get what we plan to get. That's why setting goals is so critical, the better we set our goals the more we achieve.

Often, we kid ourselves that we have goals if we have a vague idea of what we are shooting for in our heads. However, our heads conveniently smudge these ideas as soon as they become slightly difficult or another idea comes along and displaces the first. Only written goals, that have defined action plans behind them produce the outcomes that move us forward. Otherwise, we procrastinate and drift along.

When we set really clear goals that we are excited about, a strong magnet is created. The strength of this magnetic force pulls us in the right direction every day, it keeps us focused, it gives us the energy and strength to address the challenges, and overcome the obstacles that stand in our way.

It is also our engine for personal growth as the value of the thing that we have set as a goal is always dwarfed by the value of the learning and self-development we have undergone to achieve it. Goals, if they are stretching enough, pull you to become a better person, capable of performing at a higher level than you ever dreamed possible.

There are a number of ways of setting goals, all of which are valuable.

The method I have found that is most effective is described below. It is a four-step process and takes several hours. However, it produces a great set of goals that can make a significant difference to your life.

Start by listing the 6 things you have achieved in life so far that you are most proud of. These could be passing exams, winning races, graduating from university, having children, starting a business, getting married. These are things that you really remember and have a special space in your heart. For each one of these, write the emotion you felt at the moment you achieved it. Lastly, write down the driver that allowed you achieve this.

For example:

I was the captain of my school rugby team.

The emotion I felt when I was made captain was both pride and responsibility.

The driver for me was to achieve recognition from my father. He was a great player and I wanted this for him.

Your proudest achievements	The emotion you felt at the time	The driver that led to this achievement

After this exercise, you should feel proud that you have achieved so much in your life already and hence confident that you can go on and achieve so much more. It also helps you understand what drives you as a person.

Then take a piece of lined paper and make a list of 50 things that you want over the next 10 years.

Ask yourself all the things you want to do, to be, to see, to have.
Places you would like to go.
People you would like to meet.
Things you would like to learn.
Experiences you would like to have. (With whom would you like to have them.)
Fears you would like to conquer.
Achievements that you could be proud of.
Challenges that you would like to take on.

Kind acts that you would like to do for others.
Things that you want to leave as your legacy.
Outrageous fun stuff you want to do.
Beautiful things you would like to own.
Places or houses you want to live in.

There is probably a lot more. But think in terms of 'If I don't put it on this list, there is no way I am ever going to have it'. So, think carefully. Don't miss anything off.

Don't add any negative filters when compiling your list. The filters that say, 'I don't deserve this' or 'this is not practical' or 'I can't afford this'. What you will learn in this book is how you get pretty much anything you want if you learn how to, so don't be constrained by these negative filters.

You may think that 50 is a lot. It's not. When I do this exercise with children they can keep going for a long time. They are not inhibited by any negative filters: their dreams have not been dulled by life's difficulties and their imagination is boundless. As adults, we have the same capacity to imagine that we had as children, but many of us have not practised it, so now find it challenging. So, don't give up until you have 50 on your list.

When you have finished, write the number 1,3,5 or 10 against each goal. This number corresponds to the amount of years it will take you to achieve this goal.

Goal	1,3,5,10	Goal	1,3,5,10

Goal	1,3,5,10	Goal	1,3,5,10

Then sit back and review. How balanced are your goals? If you only have short-term goals, then maybe you don't have much direction in your life. If you only have long-term goals, then ask yourself if you are a procrastinator who struggles to make positive decisions and act on them.

Whatever you decide, you might want to add some more goals to balance your list. Remember the joy is in the journey not in the attainment, so don't miss out big chunks of your future by being lazy at setting yourself goals. After all, you are effectively designing your own life, so it's worth taking time and care over the exercise.

The next step is picking the four most important goals from each time segment: the ones that excite you the most. Now you have 16 big things to shoot for over the next ten years.

One Year Goals	Three Year Goals	Five Year Goals	Ten Year Goals

For each one of these, write a more detailed paragraph of what this goal is about. Describe it in detail. How does it look, feel, smell? If it's a house, for example, build a vivid picture in your description of where it is, the style, and the character of the building, the feel of the interior, the way each member of your family will use each room, the look and feel of the garden, etc.

Then write another paragraph on *why* this goal is important to you. What will it bring to your life or to the life of other important people around you? In the example above, the true meaning of the house could be around the home you want for the family you want to have; a loving and amazing environment for your partner, children and pets. This gives true meaning behind the goal, which makes it a powerful goal.

After you have written these two paragraphs, you will either be 100% convinced that this is a great goal for you. Or you may feel it's just a superficial whim that has little real substance or meaning. If the former is true, then transfer this goal into your goal book and start being the person you need to become to achieve it. If the latter is true, then discard this goal and replace it with another.

My one-year goals	Why this goal is important to me

My three-year goals	Why this goal is important to me

My five-year goals	Why this goal is important to me

My 10-year goals	Why this goal is important to me

If you have done this exercise well, you will now have 16 medium-term or long-term goals that excite you and give real meaning and purpose to your journey.

For them to become your guiding light, they will need to remain visible in your daily life. Things you don't see regularly fade quickly and the value of the powerful magnet you have built is largely lost.

Depending on how your mind works there are different ways to achieve this. Here are a few ideas that might work for you:

- Create a dream board. (A big board with images that capture the essence of your goals). Place it in a prominent position in your house, so you are constantly reminded of where you are heading. (Above the toilet is always a good bet).
- Create a goal book where you write down your goals and plot progress towards them.
- Have a goal screen saver, so you are reminded of your goals every time you switch on your PC, tablet or phone.
- Record your goals on your phone and play them back regularly.
- Write yourself a number of letters and ask a friend to send them to you at regular intervals.
- Choose whatever method works for you, but please choose one. Don't be lazy and let the enormous value of your goals fade away.

Short term goals

Our medium and long-term goals have now framed our mindset, set out the journey we are going to take and added some milestones along the way.

However, this will not help us to take the actions we need to take tomorrow to get the show on the road.

The timeframe that most successful people choose is a quarter of a year, or 90 days to set short-term goals that are both actionable immediately and contribute directly to achievement of our longer-term goals.

Three months is long enough to produce meaningful steps forward, and short enough to create a degree of urgency to get things done now, in the present, in real time.

Three is also the optimum number of goals to set. Again, enough to make a meaningful step forward, but not too much to dissipate our energy and focus across too many things that are unlikely to get finished to any degree of quality and substance.

So, setting three goals, every three months provides a ladder by which you can reach your one-year milestone, then your three-year milestone, your five-year milestone, etc.

Making your journey in bite-sized chunks really works well for managing your mindset. Often, our long-term goals seem so far away that they feel so unachievable that we switch off through lack of belief that we will ever get there. However, getting three tangible things done in three months from now, most of us can firmly grasp and deliver. You will be amazed at what can be achieved by the cumulative addition of all these three-month sprints. The compound effect of both the learning and achievements can lead to places that you struggle to believe were ever possible when you start the journey.

The importance of this really struck home for me when listening to the story of a GB rower whose career was going from strength to strength. He explained that one of the key factors to his success was his learned habit of just chipping away at small achievable goals. He explained that he was never a natural athlete and his career was slow to take root. In fact, he nearly gave up on more than one occasion. However, after a couple of set-backs, he learned the technique of setting himself modest targets that he always felt confident he could achieve. Some of the more naturally-talented rowers would set much more ambitious goals but would get frustrated when they failed to meet their own aspirations and this frustration often led to them leaving the sport. He explained that the habit of achieving his short-term goals gave him a winning mentality. He became accustomed to hitting his goals every time, which gave him a winning mindset. He expected to achieve. He expected to win.

The method I suggest for short-term goals is as follows:

Start by getting a big sheet of A1 paper from a large white board and just brainstorm all the possible things you could do over the next quarter to move you forward. Don't debate them in your own mind, just keep writing until you run out of ideas. It helps if you invite others who are close to you to join in the process. The more ideas, the better.

Then develop some criteria by which to prioritise the most important.

These could be:

- How excited am I by achieving this goal?
- How much does achieving this goal contribute to me reaching my long-term objective?
- Is the goal realistic to be achieved in the next 3 months?
- Is the goal tangible enough?
- Will I know it's been achieved?
- Will I be able to measure the result?

Once you have these clear in your head, go through each goal idea on your brainstorm chart and rate each one out of ten. Out of this, the Top 3 should emerge. Sometimes you may need to combine a couple of ideas to form one more powerful idea.

Then, we need to take this goal and write it in specific terms. This is super important as the clearer a goal is, the better chance you have of completing it.

For example:

Your goal from the brainstorm board might be: get fit enough to run a marathon.

This is not specific enough to be useful. A well-written goal might be:

Improve my comfortable running distance from 10 miles to 20 miles by the end of March and secure my place in the London Marathon.

Then, for each goal write a task list that are the smaller steps that, if all completed, will lead to the overarching goal being achieved.

These are the 'Lead' activities that result in the goal being achieved. Inexperienced goal setters tend to write goals in terms of the 'Lag' activity. A lag activity is an outcome.

In this case the Lag activity is to complete a marathon. However, in the next 90 days it's the lead activities that are crucial. We know that if we complete the lead activities then the lag goal is almost guaranteed. The trick is to stay focused on the here and now lead activities and not to expend too much emotional energy on the Lag. That will look after itself in due course.

These lead steps could be:

Book my place in the marathon.	By Jan 1st
Get a running coach.	By Jan 15th
Get a nutrition plan.	By Jan 15th
Buy new running shoes.	By Jan 15th
Increase my training distance to 12 miles.	By End of Jan
Increase my training distance to 15 miles.	By End of Feb
Increase my training distance to 20 miles.	By End of March
Run London Marathon in less than 4 hours.	April 28th.

Now we have an exciting goal and a plan to achieve it. It is now real and is something we can take action on immediately.

Exercise:

Write your goals for the next 90 days in the format below.

Goal One					
Tasks		Start Date	Finish Date	Person Accountable	Status R/A/G

Goal Two					
Tasks		Start Date	Finish Date	Person Accountable	Status R/A/G

Goal Three					
Tasks		Start Date	Finish Date	Person Accountable	Status R/A/G

Necessity Goals

A type of goal that I personally find very effective and can move you forward at a very fast pace is the necessity goal.

This is based on the human ability to achieve incredible things when they have no other choice but to do so. We hear stories of people being lost in the desert and managing to navigate to safety whilst learning to survive in an extreme climate. If this was not a necessity to survive, they would never have been able to achieve this feat in any other circumstances.

In your personal goal setting, it's possible to create necessity to summon up the levels of tenacity, persistence and perseverance required to do this.

Athletes do this all of time.

A boxer may book a heavyweight title contest in four months' time in front of an audience of 60,000 people. The minute he signs the contract, he has created a necessity goal. He has no other choice but to get fit enough and fast enough to compete and win this fight. Without this hard goal being set, he would never train at this level of intensity.

If we have the courage to set ourselves ambitious necessity goals, we can accelerate our progress. They don't have to be as ambitious as a heavyweight boxing bout but they do have to be challenging. Things that force us well outside of our comfort zone and force us to learn at a more intense pace than we would choose to take otherwise.

I worked with an Australian lady once who owned a digital marketing agency. When we were goal setting, I asked her how she would reward herself if she achieved her big goal. She told me she would take her kids for a month's holiday in Australia to meet her extended family, many of whom they had never met. I could see she was passionate about this outcome, it would mean a great deal to both her, her children and her family in Australia. I knew she was very capable of hitting her big goal, but her performance level would need to rise a level to get there. I immediately suggested we turn this into a necessity goal by announcing now to the children and the family that she was taking them on the trip next summer. I saw sheer fear spread across her face at this suggestion. 'What if I did not make it, I could not bear to let everyone down,' she said.

I asked her how much she wanted to become the mother she talked about being and whether she thought she was capable of hitting the goal. She agreed she was and reluctantly placed the deposit on the flights and told the children that very day. From that moment onwards, I knew 100% that she would do whatever it took to make it happen. Her performance jumped in proportion to the size of the stakes at play. She now travels to Australia every other year, as the performance habits she learnt during that year have taken her performance and aspiration to another level permanently.

Why not convert one of your goals to a necessity goal and see what level of performance you are capable of when the stakes are higher.

Sometimes you just have to publicly commit to do something to achieve this.

- Book yourself as a speaker at a convention in front of 800 people in six months' time and then learn how to get good a public speaking?
- Book yourself in to a marathon and commit to raise £2000 for a charity then learn how to run?
- Commit to taking a work assignment in Madrid for a Spanish company in 6 months' time and then learn how to write and speak Spanish?

Whatever you decide, have the courage to commit and the determination to succeed.

You will become a bigger and better person as a result.

Performance habits

The other type of goals that we need to become the person we want to become are our performance habit goals. Our BE goals.

These are our self-development habits that will make us a better person in relation to who we want to become.

Depending on how self-aware you are, you may well have a few of these in your mind already. They could be in a whole host of areas.

Maybe they are around:

Keeping cool under pressure.
Not losing your temper.
Being present with your partner during dinner.
Having the self-discipline to get to the gym 3 times a week.
Remembering to ring your mother twice per week.
Not taking feedback personally after a performance.

You may have your own ideas about the habits that will benefit you the most, but more powerful still are the behavioural changes that the people around you would recommend.

The people around you can view your performance from a clearer and more rounded viewpoint. They see things that you cannot see yourself; your blind-spots. If you are committed to improvement, then I strongly recommend you ask them to help you on your journey by asking their opinions.

We often call this 360 degree feedback as it seeks to involve the views of people all around your spectrum of influence: your family, your boss, your peers, your team etc.

There are many methods of asking them but a simple questionnaire is as effective as anything.

I use a pretty simple set of six questions that paint a vivid picture from which it's easy to set performance habit goals.

- What do I do consistently well in my role as XXX (father, athlete, CEO, mentor etc)?
- What do I occasionally do well in my role as XXX?
- What do I just not do well in the context of my role as XXX?
- What situations bring out the best in me?
- What situations bring out the worst in me?
- Is there any other feedback that you would like to share that would help me become a better XXX?

You can use these questions to evaluate how you are doing in any of the roles you play in life. The output from these questions can be hugely insightful and valuable.

With the many clients I have used it with, there is always a sense of pride coming from hearing what others value you for. Generally, you are held by others in much higher esteem than you yourself perceive. This gives the improvement feedback so much more credibility and value. It also builds your self-esteem. You derive a sense of desire and duty to improve for the benefit of not just yourself but for the positive impact the improvements will have on the people around you.

As with achievement goals, it's best to be working on a maximum of three at any one time to focus maximum energy on the changes that will have real impact.

In terms of writing performance habit goals, the only thing that is important is the amount of effort you put into adopting a habit on a daily basis rather than the attainment itself. As we are dealing with behavioural change, then trying your best every day is all that can be asked. This is absolutely achievable by everyone every day.

As forming habits is a function of repeating an activity over and over again until the habit is set, then it's powerful to set the target as something that can indisputably be achieved every day.

So, performance habits are best written in the format:

Did I do my best today to …?

Using our previous example, this translates into:

Did I do my best today to stay cool in pressured situations?
Did I do my best today not to lose my temper?
Did I do my best today to be 100% present with Annie during dinner?
Did I do my best today to stick to my exercise schedule?
Did I do my best today to find time to touch base with Mum?
Did I do my best today to learn from the post-match feedback objectively, without letting my emotions get in the way?

Once you have developed these questions that form your performance habit goals then ask yourself these questions every day. Rate yourself on each question, every day out of ten. If you have the discipline to do this every day, I guarantee you will make amazing progress.

However, I also predict you will fail to find the self-discipline to do this yourself daily for long enough to set the habit. It's actually really hard to do. What does work is to find someone who will hold you accountable every day for answering your habit questions. Better still, ask them to call you every day and ask you directly. Maybe set your smartphone reminder function to ask you every day. The prize that results from going to this extent in the pursuit of personal development is a big and glittering prize, so whatever accountability mechanism you choose, it will be worth it.

Exercise:

My three performance habit goals are:

1. Did I do my best today to …?
2. Did I do my best today to …?
3. Did I do my best today to …?

Weekly rating grid:

Did I do my best today to…?	Mon score 1-10	Tue score 1-10	Wed score 1-10	Thur score 1-10	Fri score 1-10

Staying focused and eliminating distractions

Writing long-term and short-term goals is a task we do on one day every 90 days. Achievement of the goals is dependent on the degree we can stay focused on these goals for the duration of the 90-day period.

Some of the regular weekly activities in your plan will become some of your High Value Activities (HVA's) and be built into your Perfect Week diary. This helps create the first level of discipline needed to keep you on track.

Discipline is the bridge between the writing of your goal and the achievement of your goal. Whilst the goal itself is exciting to us, many of the tasks required to achieve it are very mundane and often grueling. If I refer you back to the GB rower's PW diary, many or her training tasks are very repetitive, mundane and boring. They are however absolutely necessary for her to be able to perform at the highest level in her sport.

Think of the hundreds of hours of training it takes to be able to run a marathon, or the thousands of times it takes practising a kick to be able to execute under pressure at a critical moment in the match, or the thousands of hours studying case law to be able bring out exactly the right argument in court. This is the nature of becoming a high performer.

Unless you can build the habits that allow you to do this mundane work without any loss in focus and enthusiasm during the many hours that it takes, then the results will not come. You may get lucky a few times, but people who perform at a high level on a consistent basis have all learned the importance of discipline.

Discipline can be made much easier with use of a few handy tools. We have introduced the Perfect Week diary which sets us up for the week. However maximum productivity comes from the daily discipline of planning and reviewing every day. This does not have to take long. Fifteen minutes invested every day in this simple activity can increase your productivity by more than 25%. Now that's a pretty good return on investment.

This daily routine is aided by keeping a journal, either a plain old-fashioned book version or a digital version.

Every evening, before you finish for the day, spend 15 minutes working on your journal.

Start by plotting in your HVA's into your days; plan directly from your Perfect Week diary. Then think through any 'must do' tasks you want to achieve tomorrow and note them down. Ask yourself the question, 'Will it be a good day tomorrow if I get those things done?'

Daily Planner

DATE *1 / 11 /2018 /*   M T W Ⓣ F S S

▶ Things that must be done today:

1	Sign contract with AMCO	☑
2	Do Jemma's performance review	☑
3	Pay conference venue	☑

▶ Schedule:

06:00	
07:00	Work out
08:00	Breakfast with Annie
09:00	
10:00	Team meeting
11:00	1–1 Jonno
12:00	1–1 Paul
13:00	
14:00	Performance Rev Jemma
15:00	AMCO Contract
16:00	Admin.
17:00	Walk around
18:00	Planning
19:00	
20:00	Yoga

▶ Today's Frog:: *Let Emma go.*

▶ Completed ✓

▶ Other tasks I would like to do after I have eaten my frog and completed my must do's.

Book flights

Get hair cut

Thank you card Tom

Order shirts

Arrange Board Meeting

Get back to Anita

Book team away day

▶ Did I get closer to achieving my mini goals today?

✓ Yes ☐ No

▶ The best thing that happened to me today:

We signed 2 new customers.

▶ Did I engrain any new habits today?

✓ Yes ☐ No

▶ Sleep Tracker:

Fell asleep at: *10.30 pm*

Woke up at: *6.15 am*

Next think of the one thing that you really know you must do tomorrow but you really don't want to. Maybe something you are dreading. Maybe telling an employee you are letting them go, or going to the doctors for a check-up, or telling a friend that you really don't want to go on holiday with them even though you had said you would.

We call these frogs. We all have frogs and if we don't deal with them quickly and decisively, they can totally ruin our day.

The word "frog" comes from a quote from Mark Twain who said 'Eat a live frog in the morning and no worse will happen to you the rest of the day'.

We schedule the frog activity as the very first activity of the day. Mentally, this lifts our spirits as most of the time it is never as bad as what we thought it was going to be.

With a free mind and lifted spirit, we can tackle the rest of the day with energy and purpose.

Now we can complete our day's planning. Filling the gaps between our HVA's with our frog eating and getting the must dos completed.

After this, there will be a number of things you might also want to do. Some calls, some emails, some personal items. We log these and tackle them in the two dedicated half-hour time slots we allocate for these type of items. If we don't do this, then we tend to spread them throughout the day; flitting from one thing to another. This is horribly unproductive. On the other hand, if we give ourselves just 30 mins to clear our emails, VM's and phone calls it's amazing how decisive and productive you can be.

Have you ever really wanted to get to a fun event on time but know you have eight things to do before you can leave the house or office? How focused and decisive are we then?

However, if there is no imposed time pressure, how long would we spend on these eight things? Almost certainly three times as long.

Now we have built a plan for tomorrow in just 15 minutes,

This has two massive benefits.

1. You can now relax and enjoy your evening knowing that all those things whirling around in your head have been put to bed. They are captured and compartmentalised in your daily plan. Evenings are more fun and the quality of your sleep definitely improves.

2. When you start the new day, you are fully productive from the moment your day starts because you know what you are going to do and in what order. Contrast this with an unplanned day in which it's easy to spend a couple of hours chatting, having coffee, deciding what to do first, and being distracted by the needs of others, rather than owning your own day. There is no better feeling than getting to 2pm, having totally nailed all your key tasks for the day. The rest of the day is then totally yours.

The other part of your 15-minute session is a few moments to review your day. Reflect on the best things that have happened today and take a moment to smile. Without this small moment, our natural default setting tends to be stressing about the difficult bits of the day, the unsolved problems, the arguments and disagreements, the things you did not get done. Most of the time, the good things greatly outweigh the difficulties and reflecting on these gives us a positive mindset on which to end the day and look forward with optimism to a new and exciting day to come.

Also, reflect on how well you have done in adopting the new performance habits that you have been working on. This brings these habits into your conscious mind and allows you to assess your effort on these things every day. This gentle daily nudge really helps you to get just a little better every day.

If you want to start these habits straight away go to www.beperformance coaching.com and purchase a Big Wins Journal.

Deep work

Some of your HVA's will require concentrated periods of focus to produce great outcomes. Often people struggle to dedicate 100% of their focus and attention to a task for meaningful periods of time. We tend to start a task, get distracted, return to it, get distracted, return to it again etc.

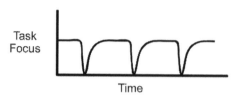

What you can see from the illustration above is that it takes time to refocus the mind on the core task every time you become distracted. Whilst we may pride ourselves on our ability to multi-task, this phasing in and out of the core task makes us terribly unproductive.

This is particularly bad if you are working in an open area with other people around. Your sub-conscious mind is keeping half an eye on what everyone else is doing and even if you are not being disturbed by them approaching you, you yourself will often pick up on something you see or hear and intervene. Having your smartphone or PC screen open whilst working on a key task is one of the biggest productivity killers today. Just scanning messages and social media content creates multiple distraction blips on the chart above and severely damages your productivity. TURN THEM OFF DURING DEEP WORK.

The idea of deep work is identifying those parts of the day where you really need to focus on an important task and put yourself in an environment where you can maintain focus for 90-minute time blocks.

For most of us 90 minutes is the amount of time we can maintain full concentration.

After this time, our mind and body need a break to refresh.

If you have a task that takes more than 90 minutes then best to schedule this in with 10 to 15-minute breaks in between. Providing you are doing something completely different in this 'break' then you refresh and can return to your deep work task with the same intensity and focus that you started with.

Deep work is highly productive and you can perform at your highest possible level during these periods.

To build deep work into your life then, schedule it into your PW diary.

Schedule it in 90-minute blocks with 10 to15-minute breaks.

Put yourself in an environment where you will not be disturbed or distracted.

Cadence and Rhythm

Building the habit of personal productivity requires a cadence or rhythm: a cycle of activity that revolves and repeats hundreds of times in order to become a habit.

The basic cycle is one of Set Goals, Perform, Reflect and Review, Set New Goal.

We have covered the goal-setting part of this cycle and large parts of the performance portion.

The essential part of the cycle we have not covered is the Reflect and Review part.

It is only by standing back and reviewing how you performed in a cycle that you can adjust, correct and improve your performance for the next cycle. This is the process in which constant performance improvement occurs.

Often, we focus our effort on the goal setting and performance parts, but don't put enough effort into designing and implementing the review portion.

Firstly, having the discipline to stop and critically and dispassionately review our own performance is a real skill. This is hard, as we are looking at this from inside out. The replay of our own performance from inside our own heads often looks very different from the reality of the performance as viewed by others who are watching the outside in view.

We can radically improve our critical review by recording our performance either with a sound or video recording and playing it back. I have done this on many occasions when trying to improve my presentation skills and coaching skills. It's pretty scary at first as I don't look or sound anything like my own self-image when I am performing. However, I see and hear things that I would never have picked up without the recordings.

For the high performance athletes that I work with, videoing their races and reviewing them afterwards is absolutely standard practice. If you think about it, this quality of feedback is not only highly valuable but it's free and easy to do for all of us. The only thing that prevents us from doing it is the chimp in our head that says 'you might look or sound stupid, so better not to look'. It's easier to stay in our comfort zone where we can imagine our performance was good and not disturb our chimp.

What is significantly easier than self-reflection is to ask for feedback from others. Having people around us who can see things we just can't see ourselves and are prepared to give us critical feedback is invaluable.

This is much easier to set up than we imagine, as if you ask someone to observe you and give you feedback, most of the time they take it as a compliment. They are honoured that you have trusted them with such an important task and you will probably deepen your degree of connectivity with them as a result.

What's even more important is setting this up in a way that it adds accountability into the cycle. For instance, if you set up a performance review meeting every month in which another party holds you to account for the performance improvements you have promised yourself, then the chances of you achieving these improvements rises significantly.

Setting up your review and accountability cycle will be a major factor in the rate at which you can raise your personal performance and productivity.

From having someone close to you ring and ask how you got on with your daily performance habits, to having a weekly review with your strength and conditioning coach, to having monthly board meetings. All these are review interventions that you can build into your performance cycles to help you on your journey to be the best that you can be.

Building these feedback and accountability interventions into your life requires planning. They won't happen by themselves unless you plan and schedule them into your routine.

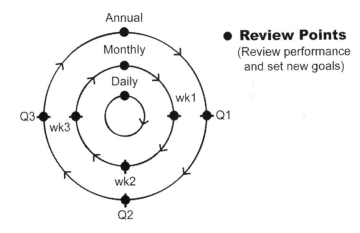

The Romans created a pretty handy time system to help with this one. They split years into four quarters. Then, they split the quarters into three months. Then split the months into 4 weeks. Then split the weeks into seven days.

The easiest thing to do is to build our review cycle into this system. Design for ourselves an annual review and reflection event, a quarterly event, a monthly event and a daily event.

The daily and weekly events may involve just self-reflection, whereas the monthly quarterly and annual events would typically be more comprehensive and involve multiple people and sources of performance data.

Exercise:

How do I review my personal performance and who holds me accountable to achieve my personal goals?

Time point	How do I review my performance	Who holds me accountable
Annually		
Quarterly		
Monthly		
Weekly		
Daily		

Getting professional feedback

If you want to maximise your rate of improvement, then one sure-fire way to do this is to increase the quality and frequency of feedback.

All serious athletes have coaches for this very reason. They are in a high-performance environment and would not dream of leaving such an important part of their development to chance.

A professional coach helps you develop your goals, provides the quality, objective feedback and holds you accountable for achieving your own goals.

Coaches are becoming a more common occurrence in all walks of life for people who want to perform at a high level outside of sport:

- Business coaches help business owners grow profitable businesses.
- Executive coaches help managers become great leaders.
- Life coaches help people improve the quality of their lives.
- Fitness coaches help you improve your level of personal fitness.
- Nutritional coaches help you eat an optimal diet for your body and lifestyle.

In the context of you achieving your ambitions the new breed of coach is the performance coach. These are men and women who understand the high-performance environment and are able to guide you to achieve your personal goals.

Clearly, deciding to employ a coach is a significant investment, but compared with other investments you will make in life the payback is always significantly higher.

It comes down to the "work hard or work smart" equation.

A coach will make sure that all the effort you put into achieving your goals is focused and productive, so you get the greatest possible advancement for the amount of time you put into an activity.

The other tremendous advantage of a great coach is their ability to keep you mentally in the performance zone. When you are working alone, your emotions often pull you all over the place. Your chimp (the voice inside your head) often tells you stories that create unhelpful emotions such as fear, uncertainty and doubt. These emotions pull you out of the calm and focused state, which is the zone in which you can perform at your optimum level.

As a coach myself, I have learnt the biggest barriers to performance are your own self-created emotional barriers, such as:

'I can't do this. I am just not very good.'
'If I try this and fail, I am afraid people will think badly of me.'
'I am too busy to do what I know I should do to achieve my goals.'
'I don't deserve to be that successful. That is for other people more talented than me.'
'This direction is tough, there are lots of barriers to overcome. I want to give up and do something easier.'

I have come to call this 'head trash'– rubbish that we all create in our heads that creates emotional barriers to our progress.

One of the great benefits of your coach is that they will listen to all the stories you are telling yourself and help you dispose of the head trash and keep you firmly in your performance zone.

Progress is a direct function of how long you stay in the performance zone. The more you are in this calm, focused and productive zone, the faster you progress.

A coach can be another of your anchors that keeps you in balance.

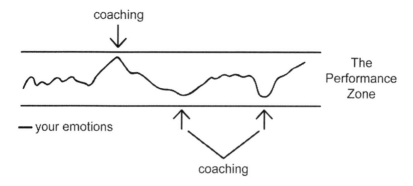

If you want to meet one of our coaches for an initial discussion, go to our website at www.beperformancecoaching.com and we will match you with the coach who is best suited to help you achieve all your personal goals.

The Language of Performance

Between you and your achievement goals there is a lot of ground that needs to be covered.

The essence of crossing this ground quickly and effectively is being guided by measuring and tracking the relevant performance indicators that tell you how you are progressing along the way.

These are the indicators that keep you focused, that allow you set milestones along the way, and tell you how you are performing vis a vis your desired goal.

Well-written goals are specific, so are written in a form of performance language.

To run the London Marathon in 3 hours and 20 minutes in April 2019 and raise £2000 for Help the Children.

or

To purchase 12 buy-to-let investment properties, producing a passive income of £6000 per month, by the end of December 2021.

The language the goals are written in is 'outcome' language. It describes and quantifies the desired outcome. This is essential for goal clarity. The clearer and more specific the goal, the higher chance there is of reaching it.

However, 'outcome' language does not serve us well in plotting our way towards the eventual goal. What we need on the way is to be tracking the key activities needed that will 'lead' to us achieving the goal.

In the first example there, it's not useful to track how fast we can run the marathon course in training, as this is not how you prepare for a marathon.

However, you might want to track firstly how many miles you can run in 45-minute training runs for the first month of training. Then, you may want to move on to track how many miles you can run in one-hour training runs in month two. Then, you may move on to the same in two-hour training runs in the final month. This 'lead performance indicator' becomes your performance language that guides you through your training.

Once established, then create your own scoreboard. The scoreboard is the mechanism that encourages you to challenge yourself and keeps the score. So, the scoreboard in this case could look like this:

	45 min	1 hr	2 hrs
Week 1	3 miles 3 miles 3.2 miles 3.2 miles		
Week 2	3.2 miles 3.3 miles 3.3 miles 3.4 miles		
Week 3	3.5 miles ☺ 3.5 miles		

In the second example, the number of houses purchased is the outcome. However, what drives this is the number of opportunities or leads generated every month. Experience up to now has indicated that on average we need to identify 45 potential opportunities in order to purchase one house. To hit the target of 12 houses in 3 years, one house needs to purchased every quarter. So, our scoreboard might look like this.

	Jan	Feb	March
Leads	12	14	16
Viewings	8	7	9
Offers	3	2	5
Buys	0	0	1 ☺

Whatever your desired outcome is, it's worth spending some quality time in figuring out what is the most important 'lead performance indicator' that you want to measure and track, so that if well executed it will certainly lead to you achieving your desired outcome. Often, it's tempting to measure a whole host of indicators, all of which contribute in some way to the outcome. This is dangerous, however, as the complexity involved means that you will 'check out' of the process because collecting and reporting the data becomes onerous, and the picture painted by the scoreboard is not clear enough, leading to a dissipation of energy and focus.

Sometimes the correct 'lead performance indicator' is not so obvious.

I worked with someone who had a contract catering business he was trying to grow. He was super-analytical and had a chart for all of his many marketing activities, his lead analysis, his website performance, etc. Pretty much everything that he could measure, he measured it. However, he was not getting the results he wanted or expected, so we set out to try and find the one 'lead performance indicator' that had the biggest impact on growing his sales. I knew that if we could find it and focus his effort on this activity, we could solve his puzzle. After lots of study and trial and error we found it.

It turned out that the type of customers that he wanted were driven primarily by relationship and not really influenced by any other type of marketing. When the business owner spent time just building personal relationships with potential clients, then the contracts followed. The only lead performance indicator we left on his scoreboard was the number of meetings the owner had with prospective clients per week. Over a period of three months, the number went from an average of two to an average of 10. His marketing team now only had one objective: to get him meeting appointments. As a result, the rate of new contracts grew and subsequently sales growth followed. We had found the lead performance indicator that drove his business.

Whatever your outcome goal is, then think hard about what your lead performance indicator is. When you find it, put it on a scoreboard and use this language to plot your journey.

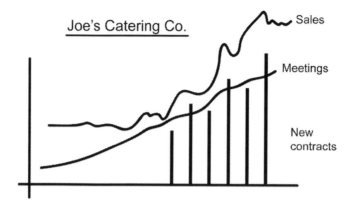

When you have designed your scoreboard, don't hide it. Make it big and colourful and put it in a place where you and the people around you can see it every day. It will give you energy and motivation every time you see it and your friends and colleagues will give you both encouragement and accountability to keep the score ticking over in the right direction. Don't put it on a spreadsheet deep inside your computer, where it takes effort to go and find it. It will not help you there.

The final part of the language of performance is the language of reward and recognition. Reward and, more so, recognition are the fuels that drive your performance engine.

Set small milestone targets along the way. Set the reward that you will give yourself and others when you reach the milestone and celebrate big when you hit it. Don't be tempted only to reward the outcome. That is not how winning habits are built. Reward achievement of the milestones along the way. This gives you a constant series of energy injections and the hunger and desire to reach the next milestone. It really does not matter how small or insignificant the milestone may seem. It is the cycle of endeavour, achievement and reward that fuels the performance machine.

Recognition is probably the most powerful form of reward. We never remember spending the cash that achieving the goal gave us, but do remember the proud look on our parents' faces when we crossed the winning line.

Recognition is also the key tool in your toolbox to keep your army of supporters engaged and aligned behind your mission. The way you say thank you makes a massive difference in how people feel about you.

For instance, if you get your PA to send flowers to say thank you to someone who supported you on marathon day, then that is a really warm gesture. However, if you write them a hand-written note telling them why you appreciate them and specifically what they did or said that made such a difference to you, then you deliver it in person with the flowers, the impact has multiplied by a factor of 10. They will probably keep that note in a drawer for many years, and they will repeat the behaviour that you have recognised because you took the time to tell them how much you valued it.

Reward yourself for every milestone along the way.

Reward others for helping you and they will help you more.

Recognise others for the behaviours you appreciate and want them to repeat.

Above all, recognise yourself for the amazing person you have become.

Exercise:

Rate yourself on the Personal Productivity Checklist (below). Work out where you are now and what you want to work on.

Personal Productivity Checklist

Areas	Score (1-5) (1 = No, 5= Absolutely Yes)
Proactivity	
Do I have balance HVA's?	
Do I have clear demand HVA's?	
Do I have clear Zone HVA's?	
Do I use a Perfect Week Diary?	
Do I reflect and plan every day?	
Do I actively avoid distraction and delusion?	
Do I practice Deep Work?	
Goal Setting	
Do I have clear 10 year goals?	
Do I have clear 5 year goals?	
Do I have clear 3 years goals?	
Do I have clear 1 year goals?	
Do I have clear 90 day goals?	
Do I have performance habit goals?	
Cadence and Rhythm	
Do I have a structured annual review point?	
Do I have a structured quarterly review point?	
Do I have a structured monthy review point?	
Do I have a structured weekly review point?	
Do I have a structured daily review point?	
Do I people set up to give me regular feedback?	
Language of Performance	
Do I have lead performance indicators?	
Do I track them on a scoreboard?	
Do I have achievement milestones?	
Do I reward myself when I hit my milestones?	
Total	

Preparing for the Journey

Now you are armed with all this new knowledge you are ready to start your journey.

Before you set off, I wanted to conclude by giving you seven final tips to help you along your way.

Tip No. 1 – Map your route

You may be asking yourself where to start. There is so much opportunity that it's easy to become overwhelmed. In common with all successful journeys it's useful to have a map to guide you.

Use this map to evaluate where you are today and start with the boxes that are going to give you the biggest wins. Score each box out of 10. 1 = I don't do this at all and 10 being = I do this and I am good at it.

As we outlined in the goal-setting chapter, only set a maximum of three goals at any one time.

Choose areas that will give you quick wins, as this will boost your confidence and energy to go to the next level.

Self Mastery

Your mind and body need to be trained to perform at your best.

Purpose

You need a strong WHY to have the engery and drive to succeed.

Score

Identity

Design your future self. BE the person you want to be.

Score

Mindset

Adopt the right mindset to perform and improve every day.

Score

Energy

Stay in the performance zone. Find the anchors to keep you balanced & focussed.

Score

Connectivity

You can't get very far alone. The art of attracting talented people to help you.

Understanding People

Understand yourself. Understand the behavioural profile of others.

Score

Curiosity

Proactively seek and engage with people to find your connections.

Score

Influence and Attraction

Tell stories that are designed to have impact, that influence and attract others to your cause.

Score

Communication

Communicate with passion and impact both 1:1 and with an audience.

Score

Personal Productivity

Getting the really important stuff done efficiently.

Proactivity

Take control of your day. Don't allow your day to control you.

Score

Goal Setting

Set clear goals that excite you.

Score

Cadence and Rythmn

Reflect and review your performance regularly. Get high quality feedback.

Score

Language of performance

Know your lead performance indicators and keep the score.

Score

Tip No. 2 – Take a guide so you don't get lost.

If you have available resources then getting a performance coach is always a great investment. They will help you navigate the journey, keep you focused and motivated to meet your personal goals.

They will know when you need support to overcome obstacles and when you need a challenge to push you to the next performance level.

Tip No. 3 – Don't listen to the naysayers.

There will be people who will be skeptical of your endeavours. Don't listen to them.

They are the people who have probably been holding you back for years; people who make decisions based on fear of failure rather than the excitement of creating success.

They will surely cast doubt on your thinking, create uncertainty about the outcomes whilst secretly wishing they had the courage to make the journey themselves.

My advice is not to enter into debate with them. You don't need to justify your decisions to anyone else but yourself.

Remember it's your story and they don't know the script.

Tip No. 4 – Find the real you.

Use this as an opportunity to be really honest with yourself about who you want to be. Time waits for no man, so don't wait any longer to pursue those dreams that you know you can achieve.

You will find a compelling purpose that will drive you forward every day if you look hard enough.

You will create an identity for yourself that is fulfilling not only for you but also for the people around you. The person that you love being. The person that others around you love you being.

Remember that superheroes are made not born. So, don't give yourself any excuses. You can be what you want you be.

Tip No. 5 – Take the right people with you.

Your journey will involve you finding many new friends and colleagues. This is part of what it takes to move forward.

However, make sure you take the special people in your life along with you. This is a journey that is best enjoyed with others. Whilst the core premise of the ideas in this book is to be proactive about determining your own future, it does not mean that others around can't do exactly the same in parallel. Your success does not come at the expense of others. Quite the opposite.

Now you know how to do it, I encourage you to teach as many people around you what you have learnt. Take them on the journey with you.

There are no boundaries or limits to how much success there is available in the world. Share it far and wide. The more you give, the more you will receive in return.

Tip No. 6 – Beware of the dangers of early wins.

When you start to get results, others will compliment you and start to recognise your achievement. This feels great but brings with it great danger. You can fall into the mindset of, 'I have got this cracked' and 'I am really good at this'.

This over-confidence often brings complacency. You stop doing those things that got you to that position in the first place and, before you know it, the wheels fall off and you find yourself back to square one.

Consistent performance requires consistent execution of the habits you have learned.

If you don't practise the habits you don't get the performance.

A degree of humility is always required to keep you grounded and in the right zone. If you stray into the world of ego, cockiness and arrogance, then a fall is on the way.

Have people around you that will keep you grounded and are strong enough to tell you if your ego pops its ugly head out – to slap it hard and put it back in its box.

Tip No. 7 – Don't be afraid of hard work.

You may have felt that the sections on goal-setting and building performance habits sounded like hard work. You were right. At first it will be.

However, I urge you to stick with it. You will not find any successful person who has not learnt to love hard work.

The trick is to celebrate every small win along the way and enjoy learning from every new mistake. Hard work is fun when you do this. The love of hard work also becomes infectious to others around you when you celebrate the wins and the learnings in style.

After a while, the self-discipline that we interpret as hard work becomes a habit in itself. At that point it stops feeling like work and becomes a positive thought. A thought that knows that the results of our new habits are rich and sweet. A thought that knows we have just made another investment in our own personal growth that will always pay back handsomely.

Finally, I want to wish you the very best of luck on your journey.

As you travel along your chosen path, I would love to hear any stories of your achievements which may help or inspire others.

If you need any other help at all, please don't hesitate to drop me a line at: david@beperformancecoaching.com

Printed in Poland
by Amazon Fulfillment
Poland Sp. z o.o., Wrocław